VERY NEAR THE LINE

VERY NEAR THE LINE

AN AUTOBIOGRAPHICAL SKETCH OF EDUCATION AND ITS POLITICS IN THE THATCHER YEARS

DONALD NAISMITH

authorHOUSE®

AuthorHouse™ UK
1663 Liberty Drive
Bloomington, IN 47403 USA
www.authorhouse.co.uk
Phone: 0800.197.4150

Published by AuthorHouse   10/07/2016

ISBN: 978-1-4772-4596-5 (sc)
ISBN: 978-1-4772-4615-3 (hc)
ISBN: 978-1-4772-4598-9 (e)

Print information available on the last page.

THE AUTHOR

Donald Naismith was brought up in Bradford in the West Riding of Yorkshire. He was educated at Belle Vue Boys' Grammar School and Clare College, Cambridge, where he held an Open Exhibition in History. After a spell of teaching at Crown Woods Comprehensive School, Greenwich, he entered education administration in Bradford. Between 1974 and 1994 he was successively Director of Education for the London Boroughs of Richmond upon Thames, Croydon and Wandsworth, whose policies helped to shape and advance Margaret Thatcher's educational reforms. On his retirement, he was appointed CBE and Chevalier des Palmes Académiques. Married with three children, he lives in France with his wife, Jackie.

Tested by these criteria I think Mr Naismith came very near the line . . .

Lord Denning, Master of the Rolls,
in *Ward v Bradford Corporation and Others*, July 1971

It remains to consider the role of Mr Naismith. As to this, I agree with Lord Denning MR that he did not cross the line between what was fair and unfair. I confess however that I should have thought it dangerous to allow any outsider to attend meetings of the disciplinary committee. It would be better if he were excluded from this committee lest he attempt to act as a member and vote. However, he did not, and nothing that he said went beyond the bounds of those matters which were obviously of vital interest to the corporation and the public.

Lord Justice Phillimore
in *Ward v Bradford Corporation and Others*, July 1971

PREFACE

Education and local government were high on Margaret Thatcher's list of matters about which 'something must be done'. Both, in her view, were not as we would say today 'fit for purpose'. Her answer to the shortcomings of the national education system was to get rid of the partnership between central and local government on which it had always been based and which she was convinced lay at the root of many of its problems. Neither central nor local government would feature to any great extent in the replacement arrangements she had in mind. In the most radical set of reforms since the Butler Act, the failed state system would be reorganised along the lines of the highly regarded independent sector whose success seemed to stem largely from the absence of both. It would be Mrs Thatcher who would finally succeed where socialism had failed, in removing the deeply rooted and damaging class division between private and state education, not by abolishing the independent sector but by extending it. In future, everyone would go to public school.

Formidable practical difficulties, however, lay in the path of Mrs Thatcher's audacious idea. How exactly were the key characteristics of the independent sector—a variety of free-standing, self-financing schools, competing for the attention of parents armed with the means of exercising a degree of realistic choice—to be introduced into the monopolistic, uniform, highly planned and regulated state system? In which event, how could fairness, an inescapable government responsibility, be guaranteed, when differences among pupils and schools were to be actively encouraged? Furthermore, the need for answers to even deeper and more problematic questions which had been kept in abeyance but which had recently been coming to the surface were taking on a new urgency: What should children be taught to prepare them for the modern world? Who, indeed, should decide what they should learn? How would anyone know how well they, their teachers, and their schools were doing? How, in such diffused arrangements, could the best use of resources, another unavoidable government responsibility, be secured? 'Relevance', 'effectiveness', 'transparency' and 'accountability' were emerging as the burning issues of the day.

Such questioning was met with fierce resistance. Over the years, teachers and their unions had succeeded in establishing the fact that 'no one except themselves had any right to a say in what went on in a school'.[1] The curriculum was a jealously guarded 'secret garden'. The ideas and practices of 'progressive' education, fused with left-wing political dogma, had established such a tyranny over opinion and comment that it was impossible to have a sensible debate about alternatives to mixed-ability teaching, child-centred learning and comprehensive schools. Attempts to do so were summarily dismissed as 'divisive' or attempting to introduce a 'two-tier' system with such self-righteous certainty that no further elaboration was thought necessary. Any challenge to the oppressive orthodoxy of the times, particularly involving the comprehensive principle, the content of lessons, selection and testing, attracted condemnation of the most extreme kind. 'For all those people trying to dispose of our schools and sell the communities they serve down the river there is a particularly low pit in hell.'[2]

In meeting these challenges, Mrs Thatcher would rely on the same policies she was to use elsewhere—the application of monetary control, free market principles and new management practices to the economy and to the public services—in which there would be no place for local government. Local councils were seen squarely as part of the problem and not the solution, to be diminished whenever and wherever possible. By setting its face against them, however, the government denied itself the contribution they and they alone could make in developing and implementing national policy as sounding boards of opinion born of experience and as test beds where new ideas could be tried out, roles which had served the country well in the past and now more than ever needed to be harnessed, not discarded.

For almost two hundred years, England has been trying unsuccessfully to create an effective mass education system, a failure in part due to wrong strategic turnings taken at crucial times, lost opportunities made all the worse for being taken by an over-centralised system. Margaret Thatcher's rejection of local government in the furtherance of her reform programme was such a wrong turning and lost opportunity.

Notwithstanding Mrs Thatcher's antagonism, many local councils, even as they were being stripped of their powers, continued to use those remaining to them to develop and improve education in their areas, often in so doing running ahead of government thinking and providing badly needed solutions, not forthcoming elsewhere, to problems which could not be avoided if her reforms were to succeed. This memoir describes how three boroughs, Richmond upon Thames, Croydon and Wandsworth, did so through their willingness to take on the 'right' as well as the 'left' wing of the educational establishment which stood in the way and, at times, to translate into action what government itself wished to do but either dared not or could not do, action which brought me 'very near the line' on more than one occasion.

Richmond published for the first time the examination results of schools in ways that enabled comparisons to be made. Ahead of the government, Croydon introduced its own 'national curriculum' and standardised tests for children at ages seven, eleven and fourteen. Wandsworth came closest to realising Mrs Thatcher's aim of replacing a council-controlled neighbourhood comprehensive system with one based on a range of free-standing, competing schools. Each of these initiatives broke new ground and was bitterly contested. Each was central to Mrs Thatcher's policies towards a greater diversity among schools and the enhancement of parental choice, which lay at the heart of her drive to improve standards and restore confidence in the national education system. As such they helped to form government thinking and to carry it into effect; all eventually found their way into legislation. Many of the papers—reports, minutes—documenting their local character and origins, however, no longer exist, a gap I have sought to fill here.[3] The changes Richmond, Croydon and Wandsworth made deserve to be remembered, not only as a matter of record; the forces unleashed by Mrs Thatcher's revolution, to which they belong, continue to shape and determine education today.

Donald Naismith
La Cavalie
November 2012

CONTENTS

INTRODUCTION

I came to office with one deliberate intent. To change Britain from a dependent to a self-reliant society—from a give-it-to-me to a do-it-yourself nation; to a get-up-and-go instead of a sit-back-and-wait-for-it Britain.

Margaret Thatcher, *The Times*, February 1984

For the poor always ye have with you.

John 12.8

Bradford: Its 'Zeal for Education'

One of the problems with Margaret Thatcher's bracing, in many ways unexceptional, even laudable, prescription was its failure to recognise how many people depended and would always depend on publicly provided services for their start in life, to enable them, in her words, 'to get up and go'. I for one never forgot how much I owed the council school education I had received in the city of Bradford where I grew up, which had taken me, like countless others, from a working-class background to university. Nor, as someone who started out on a career in education administration in its Town Hall, would I ever lose the attachment I formed there for local government as a force for good, to be enlisted, not cast aside.

At the turn of the twentieth century, Bradford was among the country's leading education authorities. One of its MPs, William Forster, laid

1

the foundations of the national education system. Bradford's School Board and later Council established an unequalled record in extending opportunities to the disadvantaged. 'A door is open in Bradford for a boy of special ability to pass right through to the Universities' was the verdict of the Bryce Commission as early as 1895. Bradford's School Board often clashed with Whitehall. Under the inspired leadership of James Hanson[1] it fought against the narrow Code which laid down what was to be taught; the system of allocating grants according to the results of tests in reading, writing and arithmetic—payment by results; and the practice of using the cleverer children to teach others. It worked hard to develop the city's elementary schools beyond the government's threadbare remit of offering children between the ages of five and thirteen an education 'suited to the condition of workmen and servants', and to establish them, in the terminology of the times, as Higher Grade Schools, offering a broader curriculum more in tune with the wider needs of all boys and girls up to the age of sixteen and beyond. From the outset of a 'national service locally administered', it seemed local government was capable of making the running. But at a cost. It was Bradford's 'zeal for education', explained a former Secretary, 'which caused the Board of Education to entertain a grudge against the city',[2] a revealing comment on Whitehall's all-too-often superior and antagonistic attitude towards local initiatives I would in time experience for myself.

Undeterred, Bradford's Council, which took over from its School Board in 1902 as one of the newly constituted education authorities established by the Education Act of that year, rapidly established a reputation for its progressive outlook. It was among the first to provide free milk, meals and medical examinations. It was the first to provide swimming pools and lessons. It pioneered nursery education and the education of children with special needs. In particular, it used its new power to provide secondary education to continue to increase educational opportunities by providing a generous number of secondary school places and, in the face of government opposition, by developing secondary education along the more comprehensive and vocational lines of the Higher Grade Schools.[3] By 1908, the ratio of secondary school pupils to the population was 12.5 to 1000, a proportion very much higher than the rest of the country. According to the Board of Education in 1908, 'The city stood out as an industrial town which on paper to all events had succeeded in establishing secondary education on a complete system and a larger scale than was usual in the country'. As the report hinted, providing places was one thing; getting them taken up was another. Secondary education was not free and was available only on the basis of competitive examination. Many parents could not afford to take up places offered or keep their children in them for the full term. Bradford bent its efforts to tackling these problems. Fees were abolished and entrance requirements loosened. Opportunities were widened for those pupils who had outgrown elementary education but who were unwilling or not able to go on to secondary education.

Progress was made. By 1926, 27 per cent of elementary pupils entered secondary education in Bradford, compared with 9.5 per cent nationally and 6.5 per cent in London. In 1929, the proportion of children admitted to Bradford's secondary schools was more than twice the national average, almost two-thirds of these from the working class, a far higher proportion than anywhere else. But in the absence of government backing, it remained an uphill struggle. Many eligible children continued to fail to take up the secondary places they had gained. Nationally, during the 1920s, more than half a million children left school at age fourteen each year to go to work.

The Bradford Trades Council had an answer as early as 1917 when, in a document that came to be known as the Bradford Charter, it called for the abolition of fees and the introduction of universal, free, compulsory education for students up to the age of sixteen without selective or competitive entry. Adopted by the Labour Party the same year, these ideas found their way into the most influential educational tract of the interwar years, R.H. Tawney's *Secondary Education for All*, which was to shape national policy. The example of Bradford's vigour as an education authority and of what could be achieved through local initiative and effort would remain with me.

Inescapable reminders of Bradford's achievements surrounded my early years. The primary school I attended had been among the earliest to be built by the School Board. My grammar school, established in response to a petition of 100 ratepayers in Manningham—an example of the kind of demand-led parent power so often talked about and

3

wished for today—had been opened by William Forster himself as the first purpose-built Higher Grade School in the country. Its founding headmaster, the remarkable Alfred Lishman, who served a scarcely believable forty-three years in the post, became a leading exponent of the higher school movement nationally and spearheaded the new authority's moves to liberalise the curriculum. His public clashes with Dr Keeling, the headmaster of Bradford's endowed grammar school—even today referred to as *the* grammar school—took on the character of a national debate about the nature of the state system. Looking out as a fledgling administrator from my office in the roof space of Bradford's Town Hall over the city's Victorian skyline, unchanged since the days of its pre-eminence, I felt part of a great tradition from which I had benefited, which I wanted to continue and, in some way, repay.

The opportunity to do so would come later, not only as the education officer of my own authority, but through my inclusion with increasing degrees of involvement in the informal arrangements Mrs Thatcher used to sidestep the civil service establishment she so deeply distrusted, particularly when it came to anything to do with education and training. I became part of the network radiating from the prime minister's Policy Unit, her press office, the Centre for Policy Studies and the new breed of 'one of us' advisors she had provocatively introduced, seeking out new ideas and feeding them back, a process which, nevertheless, in spite of its free-wheeling remit, seemed incapable of influencing Bernard Ingham's[4] characteristically blunt summing-up of many a late-night brainstorming session with captains of industry, newspaper editors and the like: 'So it's more of the same then?'

'Speak to Sir Keith . . . Speak to Sir Keith'

All my conversations with the prime minister seemed to end in the same way. Each time, I thought I was making progress, particularly on those drinks occasions after set-piece seminars. Perhaps I was. I would never know. Mrs Thatcher, basilisk, above the melee, head inclined, *intime*, attentive, for the moment all mine; I, making my case as quickly as I could before someone else cut in, searching in vain for the slightest encouragement. My time up, the hooded eyes which had been on me

4

throughout would narrow, and the non-committal voice lower to a dismissive whisper: 'Speak to Sir Keith . . . Speak to Sir Keith . . .'

Sir Keith Joseph, Margaret Thatcher's closest ideological ally, shared her thinking about the future of the education system. Both wanted to replace the collaborative, post-war, 'supply led'—in Sir Keith's stinging words, 'compulsory, coerced, conscripted'—system with one based on the more competitive, 'demand-led', consumer-friendly ideas and practices of the kind to be found in the independent sector. Education, they argued, had, like other public services, come to be run more in the interests of its providers, local councils, teachers and their unions, than its users, pupils, parents and employers. The language of the market was increasingly employed,[5] particularly by a powerful group in the Conservative Party who supported the approach of Mrs Thatcher and Sir Keith and who came to be known as the marketeers.

But if Mrs Thatcher thought that Sir Keith, as secretary of state for education and science, would make headway, she was mistaken. His often repeated question, frequently delivered despairingly head in hands, which put the government's dilemma so succinctly—'Why can't they [the state schools] be like them [the public schools]?'—remained unanswered. Sir Keith's legendary over-intellectualised approach prevented him from coming up with any practical solutions, a difficulty shared by the government over wider aspects of public policy. 'There was plenty of intellect. What there wasn't was knowledge.'[6] 'It is not too much a characterisation to say that up to the mid-'70s the left had the ideas and drove the system while from the mid-'70s as the system failed the right had all the ideas but didn't know how to apply them.'[7]

One persistently recurring idea of the right, which it didn't know how to apply, was to put the monetary value of children's education, by means of a voucher, directly into the hands of parents, empowered to spend it as they wished from among a range of competing schools. Not only would this, at a stroke, provide the means whereby all parents, not only the well-off, would be better able to choose the education they thought best for their children, but also remove the expensive and stultifying intervening machinery of local government. County and Town Halls would no longer decide which schools children should go to, nor determine the pattern of education in their areas. Free from local control, schools would be encouraged to develop their own identities better geared to the differing needs of children than the nearby 'one-size-fits-all' comprehensive usually on offer. There was no doubt about it; the voucher was the ultimate 'demand-side' weapon. Circumstances favoured its introduction. Mrs Thatcher need look no further than the large and growing surplus of school places made available by a receding pupil population to provide the new generation of schools the more varied demand-side system would need.

Although 'intellectually attracted' to the voucher, Sir Keith's kaleidoscopic mind was no match for the blizzard of practical objections and difficulties thrown up by a hostile civil service. More to the point, there was a lion in the path. The immediate state of the economy called for quick and deep cuts in public expenditure, for which there was no greater enthusiast than Sir Keith himself. Sir Keith's overriding monetarist instincts required supply of whatever sort to be brought into correspondence with demand— in education to be achieved through closures and reorganisations: 'Cuts', he declaimed, 'mean cuts—pseudo cuts of programmes or future programmes will not be enough'. The educational utopia he sought would have to be brought about more gradually and by more conventional means.

Selectivity **Replaces** *Selection*

Mrs Thatcher had less reason to be enthusiastic than Sir Keith about the closures and reorganisations now in prospect. No one had played a greater part in reducing parental choice through her removal, as education secretary, of hundreds of grammar schools, which had given generations of children of 'ordinary parents' the nearest they would ever come to the public school education they and she so highly prized—a topic most certainly not to be mentioned in conversation. Her 'marketisation' policies had more than an expiatory ring about them. Mrs Thatcher's calculation was that, given the chance afforded by her new freed-up system, aspirational parents would opt for those schools closest to the public school ideal of popular imagination, schools that offered qualities not only missing but even aggressively resisted in parts of the state system—high standards of behaviour and academic and sporting achievement, the pursuit and celebration of excellence and success, individuality, competitiveness and team spirit—qualities also badly needed in society at large. In replacing *selection* with *selectivity* Mrs Thatcher was able to confront her past record, meet head on, albeit in times of great constraint and difficulty, disaffection with the education system and begin to address and reverse some of the perceived causes of national decline.

Unsurprisingly, the teachers and their unions did not share Mrs Thatcher's analysis of the problems facing the nation and its education system; nor did they agree with her solution. They put the blame for such shortcomings as they were prepared to acknowledge single-mindedly on lack of resources. In all the many dealings Bernard Donoughue had with the National Union of Teachers he never once, he said, heard mention of education or children, only money. It was fatuous, the unions complained, to compare the performance of the independent and state sectors without taking into account the formidable advantages the independent schools enjoyed in per capita expenditure and class size, for example, not forgetting their ability to cherry-pick their pupils. There could, however, be no question of levelling up expenditure. Retrenchment was the order of the day. Mrs Thatcher had no option, therefore, but to look to the features of the public schools which would cost nothing to encourage and extend, principally, their freedom and their ability to respond to parents' wishes and priorities.

Such was the opposition even to this limited approach that, in spite of bold claims to the contrary, Mrs Thatcher's reform programme made slow progress at national level, but less so locally, where councils proved more daring and adept at venturing into the heavily mined, no-go areas of the educational landscape. It would not be until John Major replaced her as prime minister in 1990 that Wandsworth was able to introduce its new system of freed-up schools. It would be five years before Mrs Thatcher's government adopted Croydon's prototype 'national curriculum' and standardised tests, and no less than fourteen years before Richmond's publication of 'league tables' became a statutory requirement.

Whatever influence these breakthroughs came to have, was due, in no small measure, to their close physical proximity to government and a largely approving Fleet Street and I could get to the department of education and science more quickly than the creaking lift at Elizabeth House[8] could convey the secretary of state to his office on the eleventh floor. All three boroughs were but half an hour from Whitehall. Ministers could and did follow their progress easily and closely. The fact that each of the boroughs was Conservative-controlled also helped, although the claim often made that they were little more than stalking horses for governments of the same political colour was mistaken. Only in one instance was one of them 'put up' by ministers to test the water and help out. The reforms Richmond, Croydon and Wandsworth undertook arose solely out of their own conditions and circumstances and their response to the wider changes engulfing education nationally.

CHAPTER ONE

THE NATIONAL BACKGROUND

The turbulent events of the winter of 1973-4 saw much more than the decline and fall of Edward Heath as premier, more even than the demise of one nation Toryism. They witnessed also the erosion of an ethical system. Conceived in an age of intellectual confidence, institutional strength and instinctive patriotism, it was now withering away in confusion and doubt.

Kenneth O Morgan *Britain Since 1945. The People's Peace*

The twenty years I spent as director of education for Richmond, Croydon and then Wandsworth between the crisis-ridden winter of 1973-4, which marked a new low point in the country's decline, and the first signs of sustained recovery in 1994 formed a distinct—and exceptionally difficult—period in which to work. It was characterised by a public mood of self-doubt and questioning, of dissatisfaction with the usual ways of doing things which were clearly not working, and contrasted sharply with the feelings of expansion, optimism and confidence of the years that had gone before and those that were to return afterwards. Within this mood of disaffection, the forces of economic turmoil, demographic change and managerial innovation which had been gathering beforehand came together to provide the impetus, the rationale for Margaret Thatcher's peculiarly ideological blend of monetarism and free-market philosophy and the causes of its eventual triumph. In their wake, they brought seemingly endless cuts, institutional upheaval, and a thrashing around for new nostrums, however outlandish, which added to the sense of desperation.

Of all the forces at work, it was this disenchantment which was to have the greatest impact. The then prime minister, James Callaghan, had been the first to recognise its significance. In a speech to students at Ruskin College, Oxford, in October 1976, he raised the alarm about the state of the nation's education system and called for a 'Great Debate' into, in particular, 'standards of literacy and numeracy, the reluctance of school pupils to opt for science and technology', and the alleged shortcomings of 'new, informal methods of teaching', together with 'such matters as the case for a core curriculum of basic knowledge in schools, a standardised system of pupil assessment, the methods and aims of teaching including 'informal instruction', the role of the inspectorate in examining the competence of teachers, the examination system especially at the post-16 level, and the management of schools . . .'.[1] James Callaghan's list set out an agenda of educational change which dominated my years in office and which continues to the present day. As a result of the ensuing inquisition into what had gone wrong, education would be re-examined in an altogether harsher, less sentimental, more searching, more critical and more consequential light.

One thing was clear; the broadly based post-war political consensus between the major parties had broken down. The 1944 Education Act, implemented by the Attlee government, had been a Conservative measure. Edward Boyle, the Conservative spokesman, had not opposed Labour's central policy of ending selection. Such general accord was now replaced by bitter ideological warfare and recrimination over who and what was responsible for the perceived—in the absence of objective data—falling standards in academic performance and behaviour and what was to be done about them. Increasingly, unfavourable comparisons were made with the education systems of other countries, particularly those whose economies were doing better than our own and those belonging to the emerging European Common Market where the equivalence of qualifications would be important. Comprehensive education had not delivered the grammar school education for all promised in almost identical words by Harold Wilson and Edward Heath. On the contrary, the abandonment of selection had opened up secondary education to new and unsettling primary school methods and influences. Indeed, the core purpose of the national system to which everyone subscribed, that all children should be taught in accordance with their ages, abilities and aptitudes, seemed to have been swept aside without challenge by undifferentiated teaching and learning. Along with comprehensive schools, mixed-ability teaching and child-centred learning seemed to have more to do with political dogma and social engineering than the true purpose of education. As colleges and schools succumbed to unrest, in some cases out-and-out anarchy, a powerful, articulate lobby persuasively called for a return to traditional methods and values such as were recalled with affection by many of the local politicians now responsible for the education service in their areas but slipping from their control.

Education in the golden age before Crosland, Plowden and Piaget, to which the councillors looked back approvingly, had been a relatively straightforward affair—well-disciplined, untroubled by theorising and experimentation, often given in fairly Spartan conditions; plain living by no means inconsistent with high thinking. They had lined up to be let into their schools in silence and had held out their hands for inspection, one of these perhaps later to be held out again to be hit by a ruler for a minor transgression, although this, they said, had done none of them any harm. News of a parent's arrival, which spread with the speed of that of a prison outbreak, could mean only one thing—trouble. Facing their teacher in serried ranks behind bolted-down desks, they had learned to read by matching sounds to letters, to write by copying from the blackboard, to reckon by chanting their tables, and to know the difference between right and wrong at morning prayers.

Councillors now saw little in their local schools they could recognise for the better. The new open-plan spaces, in which the teacher was nowhere to be seen, seemingly lost in a scrum of noisy but no doubt purposeful activity, contrasted unfavourably with the silent, orderly, heads-down classrooms they remembered and which, they had not forgotten, could take forty pupils 'comfortably'. Now they were told that pupil-to-teacher

11

ratios of twenty to one would not do. Self-expression, they supposed, was all well and good but of little use if, at the end of it all, the youngster could not string a sentence together. Topic work and projects, no doubt, had their place, but not at the expense of a knowledge of the timeline of the nation's history and its main events, nor being able to locate Great Britain's major cities on the map, let alone those of other countries. More 'being told', less 'finding out', more application and less play, would not be amiss. Why now at Speech Days did everyone get prizes? Why was there no longer a Head Boy or Head Girl to give a vote of thanks to the chairman?

Above all, where was the money going? 'Do you know, they are putting carpets on the wall,' one chairman, returning from the opening of a newly built school confided, as if seeking an explanation for the new fashionable hessian-covered display boards. Too many young people were leaving school after eleven years of expensive education without the basic knowledge and skills to get or hold down a job—an assertion which snapped shut many a meeting about next year's estimates. Amid the annual claims for ever-increasing amounts of money, it was no longer possible to deflect local politicians' questions about the curriculum, teaching methods and standards on the grounds that these were matters solely for the profession. Tight budgets, falling rolls, and new market and management practices would put into councillors' hands the means whereby they would extract at last answers to their satisfaction.

Monetarism

Margaret Thatcher's expenditure cuts differed from those she inherited, not in terms of severity—Harold Wilson's preceding programme had been based on 'by far the largest reduction in public expenditure for a succeeding year which had ever been made in absolute or relative terms'[2]—but in the way they were implemented. In opposition, under the intellectual leadership of Sir Keith Joseph, the Tories had concluded that the conventional Treasury approach would no longer do and that the stronger measures to be found through controlling the money supply, monetarism, were needed. Now in government, levels of public expenditure would no longer be set by reference to volume—how many children had to be taught, how many teachers had to be paid—but according to the predetermined amount of money the government decided it could afford. Such was to be the main plank of economic policy throughout the Thatcher years.

During my twenty years as education officer, there was scarcely one year when the education budget was greater in real terms than the previous year's and then only marginally. Lack of money and the constant search for economies dominated national and local policymaking. Any projected increase in spending in one part of the service had to be found through savings in another. The degree of financial support local government could expect from central government was systematically reduced. In 1975, the Rate Support Grant stood at 61.5 per cent of total expenditure. By 1994, this had fallen to as little as 20 per cent. In addition, new devices to depress and control local expenditure were put in place. Mrs Thatcher's three administrations passed no fewer than fifty Acts of Parliament altering the basis of local government finance. Heads of expenditure were 'capped' and 'overspending' 'clawed back'. Reliance grew on 'specific grants', whereby money was deducted from a local council's overall entitlement to pay for 'ring-fenced', centrally directed policies and 'initiatives'. Local government was not only losing money, it was losing its powers of discretion and room for manoeuvre, a development hastened and elaborated by the introduction of new ideas and ways of management.

Management

Monetarism fitted easily and well into the Conservative government's newly found enthusiasm for management as a means of bridging the gap between ever-rising expectations and the relatively diminishing resources available, which it was now accepted would be a permanent feature of the public services. Sir Keith was an early supporter. When in charge of Health, he had called in McKinseys. In Education, he was the first to promote Business Studies in university courses. The traditional organisation of local government and education's place within it would be revolutionised by two countervailing managerial innovations: first, the devolution of financial responsibility *from* councils as closely as possible to the point of service delivery, to the schools and colleges themselves; second, the centralisation of decision-making *within* councils through the introduction of 'corporate management'.

Devolution

Unlike most of my fellow education officers, who saw their jobs disappearing, I was a keen supporter of devolution in its most extreme form. One of my most fatuous jobs as an administrative apprentice had been to authorise every single one of the thousands of items of school expenditure that flooded into the Town Hall each week to be passed onto the Treasurer's Department for payment. I often wondered what would have happened had I withheld my self-important endorsement. This was not, however, an empty power. As a teacher, I had witnessed the struggle between one of London's most talented headmasters and Divisional Office over approval of his purchase of the non-standard-issue desk he preferred.

To get rid of this kind of nonsense, Mrs Thatcher's governments aggressively advanced the tentative moves taken by previous Labour administrations to strengthen the independence of schools and colleges at the expense of local government, some of them notably pioneered by local authorities themselves: in the case of school government, for example, Sheffield; financial management, Cambridgeshire. Bit by bit, a wide range of powers over admissions, discipline, procurement, finance and personnel was successfully transferred to the managing and governing bodies of schools and colleges from their maintaining authorities now bereft of their controlling majorities. A new breed of free-standing school within the state system but outside local government, the City Technology College, was introduced. In time schools would even be enabled to opt out of local government control altogether. Responsibility for all Further Education and training was removed. During Margaret Thatcher's premiership, both local government's 'seamless robe' of responsibility for all three stages of the state education system and the 'active and constructive partnership between the Central and Local Authorities'[3] were cut to ribbons. At its end, local government was not worth the name and never would be so again.

Corporate Management

With most of my colleagues in education, I did not share the newfound enthusiasm for corporate management. Education had long been regarded as the cuckoo in the local government nest; its wings were about to be clipped. Corporate management had been smuggled into the reorganisation of local government in 1974, yet another of the upheavals that had taken place in that momentous year. At the same time as the geographical boundaries of local government were being redrawn, new internal structures were being introduced and the old departmentalism of local government swept away.

Not before time, it has to be said. The effectiveness of local government had become increasingly hamstrung by its organisation into largely self-contained departments encased in their own statutory frameworks, often led by highly individualistic chief officers. Their names were blazoned on buildings and equipment and concluded every piece of correspondence, even if this meant subordinates painstakingly copying their signatures, often with little attempt at dissimulation. The education officer's name appeared outside all educational establishments. There was no doubt who carried the can. In the event of failure—I remember the name of one unfortunate transport manager being painted out of the livery of his buses parked in their depots as he was contemporaneously being relieved of his post in one of the committee rooms—there could be no appeal to 'systemic failure', as is the case so often today. The 'joined up' government of coordination, of partnership, of liaison, of management sought by government to squeeze the efficiency it was convinced lay untapped in Town Halls went only as far as chief officers were prepared to go. Admittedly, this was no longer good enough.

Whatever the gains of corporate management overall, a clear loser was the independence of the education service which had always enjoyed a large degree of autonomy protected by statutory committees and their chief officers. Education's freedom of action was now curtailed by new committees and officers designed to implement and strengthen the coordinating role of a newly invented officer, the chief executive, with overarching if not yet overriding responsibility for all

15

his local council's activities. This found expression in one instance I experienced in a prohibition on the use of electric typewriters (except by the chief executive, of course), an embargo I got round by using one on permanent loan from the Commercial Department of the Technical College, although I had to make sure my correspondence with him was suitably conducted by means of a manual machine. He was fond of reminding us that the position of town clerk, which he had previously held, was the only one belonging to local government to be mentioned in the Bible, a surprising assertion none of us felt equipped to challenge.

Policy, Finance, General Purposes, and Resources Committees, call them what you will, came to have the last word on anything for which money had to be found; in effect, practically everything. 'Policy' proved a most elastic term. The chief executive with the electric typewriter telephoned to say that it had come to his attention that a primary school was keeping chickens. My defence that it was not unusual for schools to keep animals, rabbits, for example, elicited the deathless reply, 'Rabbits is education. Chickens is policy.'

The remit of personnel officers, initially brought in to control non-teaching staff, was rapidly extended. 'Human Resources' soon enveloped everyone. Education budgets, previously inviolate, became subject to a new corporate management tool, *virement*, whereby money could be transferred from one service to another. New battlefields opened up on every front. To the formidable service difficulties already facing the education officer was added the frustration of having to negotiate decisions which formerly had been his and his alone to make. Instead, he had to take on the time-wasting distraction of spending unproductive time in 'meetings' with other chief officers to which he could make little contribution, although everyone else seemed to have a view on what should be done with education. Education officers did not need anyone else, particularly those with flip charts, to tell them what needed to be done. Education's problems seemed fairly obvious. If anything, those charged with their solutions needed greater freedom, not less. Perversely, the cult of management, which advocated greater devolution to schools, argued for greater centralisation when it came to the place of education within local government.

Market Forces

The freeing up of schools was only part of a wider and in many ways more significant move to apply market forces to the way local and, indeed, central government was run. Once the natural party of localism, the Conservative Party had, throughout the seventies, become more and more disenchanted with local government as it steadily lost ground in local elections, failing in 1981 to hold onto its own creation, the Greater London Council. Local government was increasingly seen as obstructive and inefficient, its expenditure out of control—nothing, however, that a stiff dose of free-market discipline could not cure. Accordingly, early in Margaret Thatcher's regime, local councils were required to put a range of services—street cleaning, refuse collection, housing repairs and school meals—out to competitive tender. There would come to be nothing, not even at national level, that could not be outsourced. In future, services were to be provided on a buyer/seller divide, driven by targets and measured against performance indicators replicating the harsh realities of the world outside, from which direct labour had been unproductively protected.

How far this strategy met its own objectives, I am not able to say. My experience was somewhat limited. I was given a flavour of the new management style when one of the council's solicitors I was consulting started the meeting by making a note of the time so that I would be properly 'billed'. When I asked if I could hire—entering into the name of the game—another, possibly cheaper, solicitor, I was told I could not. Volunteering to dispense with the services of the personnel officer as an economy measure was also out of the question. My idea of moving my department out of the Town Hall altogether was equally given short shrift, although if HM Treasury could privatise its own buildings, I did not see why I should not. It seemed to me either that full advantage was not being taken of the free-market approach, which I could see had its attractions, or that the 'market' was rigged. Untouchable central establishment, back-office charges always seemed to be a bit on the high side. When the highly respected District Auditor, a byword for probity—'leave your keys on your desk'—was replaced by a firm of City accountants, I allowed myself to wonder at a 'presentation' to what extent the renewal of their contract depended on their turning in a clean bill of health, and what reliance could be placed on freelance school inspectors of all people? What was beyond doubt was the corrosive effect all this had on the ideal of public service.

The Fall in Pupil Numbers

Most significantly, one area of public policy where market forces would not be allowed to operate was the challenge posed by an unforeseen and precipitate fall in the number of pupils to be educated nationally. Against all expectations, the incremental increase in pupil numbers which had taken place since the war and had fuelled the accompanying rise in expenditure had gone into reverse. Unbelievably, the effects of the decline in the birth rate, which had begun as early as 1964 and which had continued right up to 1978, had not been noticed. This oversight enabled the Department of Education and Science (secretary of state, one Margaret Thatcher) to publish a White Paper called, of all things, *A Framework for Expansion*, countenancing a 500 per cent increase in expenditure in real terms over the next ten years. The permanent under-secretary of state, Sir William Pile, wrote, 'The last ten years have seen a major expansion of the education service: the next ten years will see the expansion continue'. Writing five years later, Sir William had to eat his words: 'In retrospect, 1977 may be seen as a turning point in education. The school population is now at its peak: it will decline for a decade or more.' It did, by a massive 30+ per cent, leaving an estimated 200,000 'surplus' places nationally, which could safely be removed, taking into account a cushion for future growth and unavoidable diseconomies of scale.

If money were to be found for the better conditions in schools increasingly called for, the dead weight of such unused places would need to be lifted through closures and amalgamations and the assets released from the sale of sites ploughed back into new buildings and facilities, a process which could not be left to the vagaries of the market but which would have to be managed through old-style planning. Comparatively few primary schools were affected, protected as they were by their need to serve smaller catchment areas than secondary schools: wherever possible the opportunity was taken to amalgamate separate infant and junior schools to remove the unnecessary and potentially damaging break at age eight.

Although concern about primary school teaching methods was growing, the most urgent priority was to sort out the more troubled secondary sector, where in many cases, Richmond, Croydon and Wandsworth included, the number of schools involved would necessitate not merely closures or mergers on an individual basis but an overhaul of the pattern of schooling to which they belonged altogether. Hard and painful decisions were unavoidable. In all three boroughs, these had been repeatedly deferred because of difficulties choosing between the alternative schemes that had become possible and the unpopularity they would inevitably incur. Nevertheless, the most immediate and inescapable problem to be tackled in each of them was the damaging effect of the falling school population and the opportunities for change which now arose, regardless of all the other difficulties closing in. Turning over possible solutions to Richmond's predicament as I drove to my new offices through the early morning darkness past giant Orwellian hoardings exhorting us to 'Put out the Lights', it felt more like 1984 than 1974.

CHAPTER TWO

RICHMOND UPON THAMES 1974-1980

Exam League Tables

This week we publish a letter from a Whitton man accusing us of suppressing figures issued by Richmond upon Thames education committee on secondary school examination results.

Mr T S Godfrey points out that a 'League Table' of local schools has appeared in a national newspaper. Furthermore, the borough's director of education has discussed the analysis on television.

In fact, the decision not to publish the very complicated statistical information was taken following the advice of the director, Mr Donald Naismith.

He suggested to the committee and the Press that because of the exceptional complications of the new system of comprehensive secondary education, the figures were meaningless and 'no value judgements' should be made from them.

Since then however these figures have been published elsewhere and have been bandied about by those fighting to save the schools threatened with future closure or amalgamation.

Because of these changed circumstances it is therefore proposed to publish next week a summary of these statistics made available to the committee.

As Mr Godfrey suggests in his letter, any further endeavour to withhold them will be looked upon as censorship.

It may be maintained by some educationalists that publishing figures of this type leads to grossly misleading conclusions being drawn. It will also be argued that exam results should not be viewed in a competitive fashion as this is damaging to the morale of less gifted children.

But the fact remains that the examination system is with us. It is universally accepted as the only successful yardstick by which to assess a pupil's suitability for a future career.

Parents and teachers do press their children to take GCE and CSE and reward them if they achieve their goals.

As a local paper, we have a duty to report on all developments, trends and statistics within our circulation area.

We believe our readers are mature enough to realise that figures can be made to prove practically anything.

And that parents are prepared to accept that a school with a low percentage of examination success may be fulfilling a role—very different—but equally important, as those at the top of the examination league.

The Richmond and Twickenham Times, 22 December 1978

Reorganisation: A Return to Selection?

Given the projected fall in pupil numbers in Richmond from some 7000 to 4500 over the next ten years, it was immediately apparent that the pattern of comprehensive schooling adopted in the expansionist times when selection was abolished could not survive. It was also far from certain that, in the current mood of dissatisfaction with education generally, the comprehensive principle itself was beyond challenge. From the borough's creation in 1965, Richmond's Conservative-controlled council had been determined to resist Labour's drive to end selection, regularly appearing in the government's 'name and shame' list of recalcitrant authorities. When it finally succumbed, it did so half-heartedly. Opinion and attitudes among party members continued to reflect the ambivalence towards comprehensive education represented at national level through their spokesman, Edward Boyle, then in opposition. Many remained wedded to the popular brand of education offered by the numerous public, grammar and private fee-paying schools within the borough and within easy reach, to which no less than 25 per cent of the pupils of the council's primary schools regularly transferred: none more so than the forceful leader of the council, Harry Hall, who ruled his party and the council with a rod of iron.

The times suited tough-minded conviction politicians like Harry. Politics had become more polarised, more ideologically driven. Long gone were the gentler days when minority parties and individuals of standing, regardless of political allegiance, might be offered the chairmanship of committees. In addition, decision-making, particularly originating from party caucuses meeting in private and dominated by ringmasters like Harry, had been enormously strengthened by the new rubber-stamping machinery of corporate management. Any sign of independence from the chairmen of service committees or their officers was quickly extinguished by the chief executive or borough treasurer. Reports would be 'pulled' before reaching the printed agenda. If one made it to the meeting, it ran the risk of being shunted off in the minutes as a 'non-reported' item. 'The chairman will say' was a not unusual curtain-raiser to many a council debate. Without Harry's support, nothing of any significance would see the light of day. On the other hand, anything with his backing, however contentious, whatever the odds, was certain to go through.

Harry Hall was not a natural supporter of comprehensive education. A grammar school boy himself, he often referred to Hampton Grammar School, indistinguishable in many people's eyes from a minor public school, as the kind of school he wanted and expected the council to provide. No official disapproval, it was pointedly intimated, would attach to me if I chose to send my children to private school. In Harry's mind, the review I was about to undertake reopened the possibility at least of a more radical rethink involving the return to selection than the conventional programme of reorganisation for which everyone was prepared. As far as he was concerned, there was no inevitability about comprehensivisation or its irreversibility.

In this, Harry was encouraged by the fact that Richmond's comprehensive system had not yet been fully implemented and the determination of the neighbouring borough of Kingston upon Thames to withstand government pressure and retain its selective schools. The new Conservative education spokesman, Norman St John-Stevas, shared none of Edward Boyle's agnosticism towards non-selective education. His active, 'hang on because help is coming', encouragement of local authorities to retain their grammar schools was to lead the Tories in one borough to stop dead in its tracks, albeit temporarily, the government's drive to abolish selection there, an example of a local authority's powers of assertion if ever there was one. Given the political will which Harry Hall had in abundance, all options were again on the table. In his room—where many such life-and-death issues were debated and decided—late at night when everyone else, even the chief executive and borough treasurer, had gone and there were only the two of us, the whisky-laden questions hung in the conspiratorial fug of Harry's cigar smoke: Where did I really stand in the grammar school debate? Was a return to selection really out of the question?

As far as I was concerned, there was no going back. Apart from the greater fairness of the comprehensive system, it seemed unchallengeable that standards would rise as the pool of talent was widened—that the pyramid's peak would reach greater heights the more its base was broadened. I shared the prevailing view that all children should be able to go to their nearest school and there receive a first-rate education. My own children would and did go to their local school, where, as things turned out, my confidence proved seriously misplaced. At the time, however, the experience of my own schooldays and as a teacher had confirmed me in the comprehensive principle. The idea on which the post-war tripartite system was based—that children could be categorised into three 'rough groupings' of differing academic propensities and matched by examination at eleven years of age to the correspondingly different schools for which they were considered best suited—had disintegrated in the face of compelling argument and evidence, which I knew first-hand to be true.

The eleven-plus was far from the objective, scientific assessment it was claimed to be. The ramshackle collection of tests I had 'passed' at age ten plus—awarding marks for mental ability, arithmetic and English as well as, bizarrely, conscientiousness, perseverance and suitability—explained how good primary schools such as mine could groom children for success and how both Anthony Crosland and Edward Boyle could claim that, given the right conditions, intelligence could be 'acquired'. The eleven-plus had less to do with identifying my aptitude for a certain kind of education than with providing an administrative means whereby the number of grammar school places available, which varied widely from area to area, could be allocated. Had I lived in a neighbouring borough in the West Riding, I might not have gone to grammar school at all. Unsurprisingly, the education many children received as a result was manifestly inappropriate. Bradford's generous provision of grammar school places for approaching 40 per cent of the primary school population explained the often-repeated criticism amongst employers in the city that children 'would be spoiled as artisans': 'A potentially good workman became an inferior clerk.'[1]

Thinking back to my grammar school contemporaries, I could now with hindsight readily identify those who were obviously in the wrong place. In addition to those like me who were 'interested in learning for its own sake'(!), were students who would clearly have been better off following more specialist technical or practical courses.[2] Leaving aside the dubious psychology and machinery of selection, the fast-changing needs of society were rendering the highly valued grammar school education increasingly irrelevant, even injurious to the nation's economic health. The education of my schooldays had not yet completely thrown off the influence of Sir Robert Morant, the architect of the modern state system, who believed 'the different classes of society, the different occupations of life' required 'different teaching'.[3] The brightest minds were now being steered into unproductive work both at school and beyond. Although I was and would always be grateful for my grammar school education, I was not unmindful of its shortcomings. I had spent my formative years within a narrow intellectual mindset and the companionship of the same sex, an experience which had left me inadequately equipped for the wider world. By playing to my strengths, my grammar school education had 'formed and fitted' me[4] for university and a job at the Town Hall, but at too high a personal cost.

In spite of the lip service paid to the importance of an 'all round' education, which the grammar school purported to give, the fact of the matter was that, as you progressed through school, greater importance was paid to those subjects at which you naturally excelled, leading to the kind of specialisation then being traduced as one of the country's besetting sins by C.P. Snow's cult publication, *The Two Cultures*. 'Arts or science?' was the question thrown at me at the 'interview' to identify my academic proclivities at the age of thirteen, as if these were not already well known. I was not even asked to sit down. Thereafter, all science and practical subjects were dropped. Only mathematics survived. German was added to French and Latin, and twice as much time allocated to English, now divided into Lang. and Lit. At the time, all this suited me down to the ground, but later I was to regret the opportunities and experiences closed off to me. I wished more care and time had been taken over those studies I found uncongenial and difficult. But that was not the grammar school way. Ability was coached and inability allowed to coast. At the first swimming lesson, those who could already swim were herded to the deep end where they were to be intensively trained for medals. Those who could not, like me, were left to flounder in the shallow end, where many of us remained. I never learned to swim all the time I was at school, albeit that the swimming baths we used were commendably the first in the country particularly provided for school use.

For all these reasons, whatever shape the future pattern of education in Richmond would take, I was sure it should be non-selective, although the comprehensive plan I inherited had not been fully realised. The intention had been to create a network of well-resourced, comparable neighbourhood schools each for approximately 900 pupils between the ages of eleven and sixteen, leading to two sixth-form colleges. The abolition of selection, as with other similar major education innovations, had, however, been more concerned with the acceptance of principle than its implementation in practice. Richmond had had no alternative but to base its new all-ability system on the buildings it inherited from the previous and different educational patterns of the former Surrey and Middlesex County Councils out of which it had been formed. As a result, wide and indefensible variations in the facilities and learning opportunities comprehensivisation was meant to expunge continued to flourish, inequalities which the impact of falling numbers could only make worse. Schools based on the better equipped former grammar schools outperformed those which had their origins in secondary moderns and were more popular. Few of whatever provenance had reached their planned optimal size; some because of site restrictions, regardless of the availability of finance, never would. The Church schools were impractically small.

Size was an important element in planning all-ability schools and aroused strongly held differing opinions. If comprehensive schools were to continue the grammar school tradition, not to mention extend it as promised to those who had previously missed out, they would need to be large enough—first, to ensure that all pupils could be taught in groups according to their abilities and, second, to yield enough pupils wishing to stay on to create a viable sixth form, for many parents and politicians the guarantee and touchstone of academic standards. Received wisdom about the best size for a comprehensive school ranged from a minimum of a total enrolment of 900 pupils, Richmond's chosen model, to 2000-plus preferred by the country's largest and most influential authority—the one most ideologically committed to the success of the comprehensive ideal—the Inner London Education Authority,[5] which went so far as to contend that a comprehensive school with fewer pupils and without an intake reflecting the population's range of ability could not fully realise the potential of a truly comprehensive education, an argument with which I did not agree and which was to prove fatal to its cause.

The six years I spent teaching at one of London's latest state-of-the-art, purpose-built comprehensives, Crown Woods, whilst confirming my preference for comprehensive over selective education, alerted me to the dangers of excessive size. The 'essential' streaming and setting insisted on by Anthony Crosland no less, and which Crown Woods' roll call of 2000-plus was specifically meant to protect was, to my dismay, soon abandoned, aggravating size-related problems of discipline and organisation which would eventually lead to the school's closure. Even in my time, convoys of lorries would arrive at the end of the school year to cart away mountains of broken chairs, desks and equipment. At their respective retirements, it was the caretaker not the headmaster who went to the Palace. Schools of 900, on the other hand, would allow differentiated teaching but within a more human scale and environment. The inability of such schools to sustain viable sixth forms was not a consideration facing Richmond, which had already taken the hard decision to hive off and concentrate sixth-form studies separately in two sixth-form colleges.

If Richmond's comprehensive scheme was to be implemented as originally intended, a drastic reappraisal of the borough's educational building stock would need to be undertaken to ensure it was being used to best effect; inadequate sites and buildings closed down, put to other uses, or sold to release 'off-programme' money, which would not otherwise be available, to be invested more advantageously elsewhere. Looking up from the drawing board, however, brought us face to face with two perverse but unavoidable conclusions. In order to achieve our goal, we would need an alternative to the widely respected grammar school-based pattern of post-sixteen education, and we would need to close the 'best' school in the borough, Twickenham County Girls' School. Based on the former prestigious grammar school of the same name, still with a sixth form, it came closest to the kind of school a weighty measure of public opinion in the borough wanted to see made available to everyone, not removed. It was, indeed, the kind of school the education spokesman for the Conservative Party, Margaret Thatcher, then in opposition, had made no secret of wishing to preserve.

The Tertiary College

Given the sulphurous atmosphere of speculation about reorganisation and public hostility to the first raft of expenditure cuts, and with local elections in the offing, the future of Twickenham County Girls' School and the issues surrounding single-sex education generally were far too contentious to be tackled straight away. These would have to wait. The future of the two sixth-form colleges, however, which held the key to the wider secondary school plan, need not, indeed could not, be postponed. My proposal was that they both amalgamate with the Twickenham College of Technology on its central and generous site to form a new kind of Further Education college which had begun to make its appearance in other parts of the country, the tertiary college, so called, somewhat bleakly it has to be said, because its mix of vocational and academic courses aimed to meet the needs of most young people wishing to continue their education beyond the secondary stage.

The particular circumstances of Richmond's education system then prevailing were strongly suited to the establishment of such a college. Although the sixth-form college serving the Middlesex side of the borough, Thames Valley, was fully subscribed, the one on the Surrey side at Shene was well below its intended capacity and not likely to survive. The Twickenham College of Technology had not yet found a role in the changing Further Education scene. The government had rejected an earlier proposal to merge it with the nearby Maria Grey College of Education. The amount of its advanced level work was falling, and its position was weakened by lack of leadership. The principal had left under a cloud, and one of my first actions had been to dismiss the registrar, a move which led to an important High Court action. For those interested in the relationship between master and servant in the twentieth century, *Gunton v London Borough of Richmond upon Thames* (1980) is required reading.

In purely material, organizational terms a new tertiary college along these lines would not only resolve the future of these three institutions but, by concentrating facilities and personnel in one powerful centre, solve one of policy's current conundrums—how can services be improved and expenditure reduced at the same time? Through the better use of resources in this way, the limitations of the sixth-form college, restricted by regulations to academic subjects, would be removed and educational opportunities for school leavers greatly enhanced. I was enthusiastic about the tertiary idea. Such a college provided not only a better transition between compulsory and voluntary education but a bridge across so many of the other fault lines of our education system—the damaging distinctions separating education from training, liberal education from specialisation, academic from vocational study, full-time from part-time courses and the world of study from the world of work. For teachers, such a college would provide unrivalled opportunities to develop new interdisciplinary courses, particularly across the artificial arts/science divide, fusing the applied with the abstract, practicality with creativity, and so offer, through a greater spread and combination of options, a range of choices better suited to the varying abilities and aptitudes of students. When responsible for Further Education in Bradford, I had amalgamated Bradford's Technical and Art Colleges for the same reasons and with the same high hopes, which as far as I could see, had largely been fulfilled.[6]

For the students themselves, the tertiary college would provide a more adult environment in which they would be brought to an awareness of the different educational and vocational routes each could follow. There could only be advantage in those heading for university rubbing shoulders with those already in employment, paying their taxes and choosing to study part-time and, of course, vice versa. Young people were growing up faster, a fact recognised by the recent lowering of the age of majority. A place of learning more attuned to the realities of adolescence and the outside world would, I believed, stand a better chance of encouraging young people to continue their education beyond the age of sixteen than the expectation that they continue in the same place they had entered as different people aged eleven. In deploying these arguments, I was all too aware how firmly my advocacy was rooted in my own highly specialised grammar school education and restricted sixth-form experience. The tertiary idea offered a new departure towards a better education after school, more intelligently and sensitively organised. It was a departure I sought and wanted others to take.

The reorganisation scheme to be put before the council involved: the amalgamation of the two sixth-form colleges, Thames Valley and Shene, and the Twickenham College of Technology on the site of the College of Technology to create a new tertiary college there; the establishment of a new up-to standard secondary school in the premises of Shene's vacated sixth-form college in place of two small schools, Barnes and Gainsborough, which would close, and the transfer of Kneller Girls' School to the better site and premises of the vacated Thames Valley sixth-form college. In a separate but parallel and greatly underestimated development, the borough's two small denominational schools, St Mary Magdalene Church of England School and St Edward the Confessor Roman Catholic School, which shared adjacent sites, agreed to amalgamate to form a new ecumenical school to be called Christ's. Badly needed new 'off-programme' money, released as a result, was to be spent on improvements at the tertiary college, the new Shene School, and two of the schools unaffected by reorganisation, Rectory and Grey Court. This time round, there was no money for the borough's other secondary schools, Teddington Boys' and Twickenham County Girls' Schools, over which there were question marks, Whitton and the newly-built Orleans Park.

By agreeing to this strategy, Harry Hall would trade off acceptance of the comprehensive principle dear to the 'left' for the economies the 'right' demanded. In the event, the economic situation had not allowed any serious re-examination of a return to selection. The need for immediate savings was urgent. The education estimates were the determining factor in setting the level of the annual rate. As a businessman as well as a politician, Harry knew about rates. For the first time, he told me, they were threatening to outstrip rents. The government's decision to cut 2 per cent from public expenditure instead of proceeding with a 2 per cent projected rise had been reflected in that year's Rate Support Grant settlement, on top of which the teachers had just received a 29 per cent pay rise. Harry was not, however, unmindful of wider educational considerations. He went to Exeter, where the country's first tertiary college had been set up, and insisted on speaking to students privately. The removal of almost a third of school places would bring with it considerable political risks and, as things turned out, consequences. Nevertheless, certain of the rightness of the course of action upon which he had decided, Harry, with admirable courage, drove the scheme through his party. The much more difficult challenge of facing the public fell to the chairman of the education committee, Arthur Alcock. No one could have been better suited to the task.

Although Arthur Alcock's Toryism was firmly rooted in the liberal, pragmatic tradition of his party, there was nothing wet or woolly about his approach to politics. A successful businessman in his previous professional life, he was as hard-headed as Harry Hall when it came to the financial facts of life. But, more open-minded and by nature conciliatory and consensual, Arthur was better equipped to bear the brunt of the hostility aroused by the unfolding effects of the cuts on the education service: job losses, larger classes, the abandonment of pre-school education, higher fees for adult education, fewer materials and less equipment; for the first time, money had to be borrowed to buy books. He never lost sight of their impact on people. Of particular importance, teachers trusted and respected him. They knew that, in spite of all the current difficulties, he wanted the comprehensive system he had so powerfully helped to introduce to succeed for the very best of reasons. They also knew that he saw the tertiary college, whose cause he had wholeheartedly espoused, as further extending opportunities to those who tended to lose out in England's class-ridden educational system, for whom he had an instinctive sympathy. In his dealings with the borough's teachers Arthur was greatly helped by the understanding and leadership of David West, the headteachers' spokesman and Norman Radley, the Secretary of the local branch of the NUT. The alliance he shrewdly formed with the most effective pressure group in the borough, the Campaign for State Education, the guardian of the comprehensive ideal, led by the incomparable Joan Sallis, ensured a less hostile reception from parents and the public than would otherwise have been the case.

Opposition

Opposition in the council, sharpened by the imminence of local elections, came from the two minority parties, the Liberals and the Labour Party. The fortunes of the Liberals were on the way up; those of the Labour Party on the way down. The easy target chosen by the Liberals for their assault was the statistics on which the reorganisation plan was based. These were exceptionally difficult to construct. If the Registrar General could get them wrong, what chance did we have? To forecasts of future fertility and birth figures were added the complications of trying to pin down a fluctuating adult population in a compact area of south-east London accustomed to the ebb and flow of children criss-crossing borough boundaries. The statistics provided the Liberals with endless openings for challenges, calls for further 'clarification' and reports, anything to put off a decision. Their leader often slyly referred to 'Mr Naismith's slide rule'. No one had a greater stake in the reliability of the figures than myself. A top priority was to safeguard the borough's schools from another such upheaval for as long as could be foreseen. A reorganisation on this scale could be justified only if based on the soundest of calculations. These were expertly constructed by Richmond's deputy, Peter Waters, who possessed, along with so many other qualities, a brilliant mathematical mind— and our secret weapon, a computer. His projections were impeccable and would be borne out by events.

Principled opposition came in the elegant and formidable shape of Geoffrey Samuel, leader of the Labour Group. What his party lacked in numbers—it lay third behind the Liberals—was more than compensated by his powerful skills of advocacy. He marshalled his arguments with the surety of a first class barrister and delivered them with the greatest aplomb. Speaking without notes—a facility which never seemingly ceased to amaze his fellow councillors and which lent certainty to his case—he argued to devastating effect in complete control of his brief and audience. In attacking the reorganisation plan, Geoffrey spoke not only out of intellectual conviction but with authority as the head of a comprehensive in a tough part of Hounslow, where he had successfully brought the varying needs and interests of his pupils within the enclosing ethos of the grammar school, for which he was an uncompromising and unapologetic champion. Ideally at the reorganisation debate, he would have wished to have been defending the place of the sixth form in the education system. Instead, the sixth-form colleges would have to serve as proxies. His argument went along the following lines

> The education offered in sixth forms and in the sixth form colleges belongs to the well-established and highly regarded grammar and public school tradition of education, a byword for excellence throughout the country and abroad. It teaches young people to the highest academic standards required for entry to the universities and the professions. In addition, it prepares them for life through a rounded education aimed at developing character and interests beyond their immediate studies. Arguments that the tertiary college would represent a better use of staff especially in shortage subjects are misplaced. Many such staff are attracted by the prospect of teaching in sixth form conditions which should be preserved as an important factor in recruitment to the borough. A sixth form education has provided generations of young people, particularly those from disadvantaged backgrounds, with the opportunity to reach the highest standards of personal and professional success. It will not be possible to offer such a distinctive and coherent educational experience in the tertiary college; the college will be too big, too impersonal and too disparate in its composition. The great majority of its students will be following part-time as well as full-time, self-contained courses focused on the grades and qualifications immediately needed for their chosen employment. Academic and vocational education are two different things. Academic education is concerned with broadening the mind through study and reasoning. The aim of vocational education—training—is to refine practical skills through the application of ever-narrower techniques. The tertiary college is an experiment. We are in danger of replacing a tried and tested method of education with one we

cannot be sure will be an improvement. The tertiary college will monopolise post-sixteen education and so remove from students and parents who depend on the state system a valuable and valued choice. Establish a tertiary college by all means, but as an additional alternative to other forms of post-sixteen education to create the wider range of choice in the borough the Conservative Party says it wishes to promote.

Ouch. This would not be the first time the Conservative Party had covered itself with the mantle of reform, leaving the Labour Party to defend the status quo. Many of the Conservative front benchers agreed with much of what Geoffrey Samuel said.

However clear-cut the case for closing or reorganising a school, however sensible its place in the overall long-term scheme of things, however generous and thoughtful the transitional arrangements, nothing can be said or done to lessen the opposition such proposals inevitably provoke. On paper, in the office, or being explained to a committee, closure or reorganisation proposals would be models of compelling reasonableness. At public meetings, however, night after night they aroused visceral incredulity, scorn and anger, no matter that the schools in question might have been the object of well-founded, age-old criticism and lack of support from the very people now coming to their defence. The statistics were unfailingly wrong; the advantages claimed for change were always exaggerated or dishonest; and the motivation again was unsullied cost-cutting, not the welfare of pupils, who were little more than guinea pigs in yet another educational fad. After one parental confrontation, I asked Arthur how he had got on. 'There was hatred in their eyes, hatred,' he replied. At the next election, Harry Hall was to lose his seat and the Liberals to come dangerously near to the control they would eventually take, a proximity which was to leave the fate of the next round of reorganisation perilously dependent on a single vote.

In its planning stages, the tertiary college had the enthusiastic backing of Gerry Fowler the minister of state for further education. Once approved, it was opened by the secretary of state herself, Shirley Williams. An early visitor was the minister of education for China no less. Across the shiny, flag-bedecked table, Harry Hall and Arthur Alcock, life-long stalwarts of the political 'right', expounded the advantages of breaking down the barriers between brain and brawn, full-time and part-time students, and so on and so forth. The minister dutifully expressed admiration. How he wished he could follow us down this truly communist path. But alas, given the huge numbers he had to cope with, if his country were to make the giant leap forward, its education system would have to seek out and cultivate the most able. He was in the United Kingdom to study methods of selection; a piquant sweet and sour situation. At least Richmond's cultural revolution in this respect had been achieved.

The Publication of Examination Results

'Value for money' and the effectiveness of comprehensive education had been major preoccupations for Harry Hall in weighing the pros and cons of the reorganisation scheme and were to loom large in any significant discussion affecting education generally. It was increasingly difficult to argue education's corner for more resources without evidence of what the ratepayers were already getting for their money and whether, as claimed, comprehensive education was indeed producing better results. Teachers were becoming more militant, ready to 'work to rule' or strike at the drop of a hat. And they were beginning to get pay settlements more usual for those workers with more obvious industrial muscle. As a result, their performance was coming under greater scrutiny. At a 'Great Debate' meeting in Richmond—one of a series nationwide—the crowded hall soon showed its impatience with the lofty *tour d'horizon* offered by Shirley Williams and the platform party from Westminster. The first question from the audience: 'Why hasn't my son's homework been marked for the last three weeks?' was aimed at me.

Independent schools, Harry Hall somewhat disingenuously pointed out, had no problem parading their examination results. I was in no doubt that the council's secondary schools would have to do the same if we were to gain parents' confidence and retain a greater number of primary school pupils within the state system, which would be a future measure of our success. It was to my mind no longer possible to put off attempting to confront the criticism that the abolition of selection had led to a fall in standards and that the performance of non-selective schools could not stand comparison with the independent sector. In spite of the instinctive antagonism by supporters of comprehensive education towards anything that smacked of measurement, better information was called for and rightly so.

Although schools referred to their examination results on Speech Days and in their brochures, they did so fleetingly and, understandably, in ways that cast them in the best light. A good batch of results was put down to good teaching, poor results to 'a poor year's intake'. As things stood, there was no way an opinion could be formed as to how well schools were doing in relation to each other or against any objective test. At one of my very first committee meetings I discovered, to my disbelief, that in a report on examination results, the names of the schools had been blanked out to 'protect' them. Much of the evening was taken up by farcical attempts to guess the schools referred to. The heads and teachers generally, supported by their unions at national level, resisted letting me have their results in the standardised form I sought and which I considered the minimum requirement if any kind of realistic attempt were to be made to assess the relative performance of schools. In their view, however, it was not their pupils who were being tested but themselves, which of course in a way and to some extent, it was. When I pressed the DES for an explanation why the government supported the teachers' withholding examination results, I was told, 'Because you are going to use them'.

Newly introduced Articles of Government, ironically meant to give schools greater independence from the Town Hall, had, however, not only laid on schools the duty of providing the education officer with such information as he might require, but *in such form* as he might require. I was going to get my way. Leaving aside the contribution access to tables of standardised results would make to the new, more open relationship between politicians and the profession I thought necessary, there was another reason for making comparable results easily available. The old proximity rule guaranteeing places at the local school had been replaced by a new system, whereby places would be allocated according to the preferences parents made. An unacknowledged but nonetheless real element of unaccustomed competition was creeping in for the first time. The proportion of parents getting a place at their school of first preference was to become an important indication of a local authority's own performance, which would be watched closely. If parents were to exercise a 'choice', as the politicians insisted on calling it, it was clearly important that they be enabled to make an informed choice. It was becoming less acceptable to advise parents to undertake an exhaustive tour of schools and compare their 'ethos'. Harder evidence was called for and in user-friendly form.

There were many reasons why the publication of league tables would not, in itself, be the answer. The public examinations taken, it was contended, did not reliably measure effective teaching and learning, although no credible alternative measures which did were ever forthcoming from this source of criticism. So many variables were involved over which schools often had little control, principally the ability and motivation of their intakes, that fair comparisons were not possible. If the more worthwhile exercise of an assessment of the educational value a school added were to be attempted, it would be necessary to know more about their pupils at the beginning, reawakening the spectres of ability-testing, selection and differentiated teaching thought finally exorcised. Unsurprisingly, Richmond had abandoned the collection of this kind of information when selection was abolished; the baby had gone out with the bathwater. In any case, examination results told only part of the story. Valiant and important work on behalf of non-examination pupils would be devalued and go unrecognised. The publication of such results against a background of falling numbers when decisions had to be made about which schools should close and which remain would only serve to strengthen the more popular schools to the detriment of the weaker. Inequalities would be widened.

There was one criticism which I felt was of overriding importance: the fixation on published examination results which would inevitably arise in the emerging competitive environment would distort teaching and be inimical to education in its profoundest sense; what was most valuable in education was immeasurable. In the event, this apprehension proved well founded. Schools and teachers did allow good practice and the interests of children to be subordinated to the improvement of measured performance, particularly with the later introduction of targets, in the government's hands a wholly unnecessary and regrettable development which I had not foreseen. I for one naively and greatly underestimated the degree to which professionalism would allow itself to be prostituted for the sake of statistical advantage.

Each of the arguments against the publication of examination results had force and deserved a considered response. In aggregate, however, they added up to the contention that the layman could not be trusted and that information should therefore be deliberately withheld, an insupportable position for any public service but particularly for the one devoted to knowledge and enquiry. And in a world at the start of the information revolution it was futile to argue that members of the public, many of whom in their private and working lives managed data of equal or greater sophistication, could not properly handle published examination results, although, unfailingly, each year I had to remind committee members comparing one year's results with another's that they were not dealing with the same children!

In presenting the examination results to the education committee, I went to great pains to hedge them about with every conceivable qualification against misinterpretation, so much so that I was held responsible by the local newspaper, *The Richmond and Twickenham Times*, for its astonishing decision not to publish the examination results at all(!), a decision rapidly reversed following a protest from one of its readers; an early example of parent power, transparency and accountability with a vengeance. For the first time anywhere in the country, parents had a bird's-eye view of the examination performance of all the state schools in their area. Tables showed, in standardised form, the number of boys and girls of examination age in each school; the number of them entered for public examinations, subject by subject; and the grades achieved, expressed as a proportion of each category. 'Crude but effective' was the verdict of the headmaster of my son's school. In a government consultation paper, Shirley Williams, alas forever in thrall of the unions, issued a rebuke, ' . . . league tables based on examination or standardised tests in isolation can be seriously misleading'. Of course such information needed to be refined and supplemented. And so, over time, it was, as the market philosophy gained ground, although the government's requirements initially laid down in 1991 were substantially the same as those Richmond had used no less than fourteen years earlier.

The Closure of Twickenham County Girls' School

One school which had no difficulties with the publication of examination results was, not surprisingly, the one with the highest scores and, in the opinion of many, quite simply the best state school in the borough, Twickenham County Girls' School. Unfortunately, it was one of the three single-sex schools which cut across our plans for a network of neighbourhood schools and which did not, in any case, taken together reflect the overall pattern of parental preference. Although there was certainly a strong demand for all-girls' places sufficient to support one 900-plus school, there was no discernible demand for the all-boys' places provided by Teddington Boys' School, which was not centrally placed and so deprived a well-defined area of a local school both boys and girls could attend. Furthermore, the imbalance between single-sex places, particularly the preponderance of all-girls' places, distorted the curriculum of the borough's co-educational schools; a fairly abstruse consideration, which in previous times would not have attracted much attention, but which had come more to the fore as a result of heightened awareness of equality issues stemming from the recently passed Sex Discrimination Act. The proposal to turn Teddington Boys' into a co-educational school aroused little interest. In contrast, the proposed amalgamation of the two all-girls' schools, albeit on the better Kneller site, unleashed the most ferocious opposition, centring on a parental campaign to 'Save Twickenham Girls' School'. For many people in the borough, not only parents, its closure was a step too far.

The political task of pushing this scheme through the council fell to John Baker, the new leader in place of Harry Hall, who had lost his seat, and John Lambeth, the new chairman of the education committee, who had taken over from Arthur Alcock. The national political scene was also changing. The reorganisation plan had been published early in 1979 with the aim of being implemented at the beginning of the following academic year. As usual, the scheme had been rehearsed with the DES, and we could be reasonably certain of a favourable decision from Shirley Williams. But support for the Callaghan government was ebbing away. In May 1979, it was replaced by what was to be the first administration of Margaret Thatcher, who as shadow education secretary had actually written to the parents of Twickenham County Girls' School pledging her support!

This national development did nothing to help John Baker and John Lambeth, who had a first-class rebellion on their hands. Fortunately, they were more than equal to the task. To the very last minute, however, it was uncertain whether the reorganisation plan would go through. Failure would have represented an unprecedented defeat. The mayor, who would have the casting vote if it came to that, infuriatingly refused to commit himself one way or the other, keeping everyone literally on the edges of their seats. One permitted abstention on the Tory side, and the mayor finally coming into line at the very last minute, but not before a seemingly interminable wait, saved the day. The reorganisation scheme was approved—twenty-five in favour, twenty-three against.

But we were not out of the woods yet, not by any means. What would the new secretary of state, Mark Carlisle, decide in view of his prime minister's well-publicised support for the school? The lobbying intensified. The national press began to follow the story. I had been tipped off by the official in charge of the approval process that the government was 'minded' to agree to Richmond's proposal. So too, alas, from another source had *The Times*. To my dismay, I read on its front page the next day a prominent report of the likely 'decision' provocatively presented as an indication of the direction we could now expect education policy to take in spite of undertakings given to the contrary beforehand by no less a person than the prime minister herself. To compound my anxiety, my friend at the DES telephoned to say that Lady Young, the minister immediately responsible for the decision and a close confidante of Mrs Thatcher, had, in view of *The Times* report—which he had felt himself duty bound to draw to her attention—sent this hot potato back up to the secretary of state himself. One of the few saving graces of Regal House, which housed the education department in those days, is 'The Rugby Tavern' on its ground floor and to which I repaired to down a pint and watch the snow falling. It was getting colder by the hour. I need not have worried. When the call came, it was to say that the pragmatic and sociable Mark Carlisle had not only approved the scheme but had apologised for letting slip at a party his intention to do so. I felt I had come very near the line again.

Apart from Twickenham County Girls' School, another school not overly concerned with the publication of examination results was the Junior Department of the Royal Ballet School, whose presence in the borough was largely unknown. I came to know it well as the secretary of state's representative on its governing body. Then housed in the Palladian splendour of White Lodge amid the green fastnesses of Richmond Park, it was off the beaten track educationally as well as geographically. It broke all the conventions of mainstream education. Here boys and girls between the ages of eleven and sixteen were intensively trained to the highest international standards in one of the most specialised forms of dance, the ballet. At the same time, they followed a general education leading to the usual range of public examination subjects. The school seemed to have sidestepped many of the conundrums that tied the designers of the state system in knots. It made a great impression on me. Within its walls were played out as, in a *pas de deux*, the two opposing and unresolved themes of our education system—on the one hand, our wish that all children should receive a broadly based, rounded, liberal education through their introduction to the widest range of knowledge, skills and understanding and, on the other, that they should be enabled to reach the highest levels of personal and professional achievement through cultivating the special talents and enthusiasms each one has. This tension between the common curriculum and specialisation would dominate policymaking during my time at Croydon. But first there were the all too familiar problems caused by falling numbers to be tackled.

CHAPTER THREE

CROYDON 1980-1988

Junior Stage 8-11

At the end of this stage of education, the majority, about 75% of children should be able to:

a) describe, identify, discriminate, sort and classify objects;

b) recognize simple numerical and special relationships;

c) use number in counting, describing, estimating and approximating;

d) appreciate place value, the number system and number notation, including whole numbers, fractions, decimals, and bases other than 10;

e) appreciate the connection between fractions, decimal fractions, and the most common percentages;

f) appreciate the measures in common use; sensibly estimate and measure (using scales and dials) length, weight, volume and capacity, area, time, angle and temperature, to an appropriate level of accuracy;

g) understand enough about money to carry out simple purchases;

h) carry out practical activities involving the ideas of addition, subtractions, multiplication and division;

i) perform simple calculations, involving the mathematical processes indicated by the signs +, - , x, /, with whole numbers (maintaining rapid recall of the sums, differences and products of pairs of numbers from 0 to 10);

j) carry out with confidence and accuracy simple examples in the four operations of number, including two places of decimals (as for pounds and pence) and three places of decimals (for kilogrammes and grammes) appropriate to the measures used;

k) approximate and check whether the result of a calculation is reasonable;

l) multiply and divide numbers up to two decimal places by 10 and 100.

A Statement of Policy by the Education Authority on the curriculum followed in primary and secondary schools in Croydon, April 1983, adapted from the Cockroft Report, *Mathematics Counts*

Reorganisation—Again

Arithmetic of an altogether more immediate, less academic kind showed the extent of the damage being inflicted by falling numbers on the school system in Croydon, greater than that in Richmond, in fact one of the most severe in the country. School building had kept pace with the town's rapid recovery and expansion after the war. With demand now going into sharp decline, it was estimated that some 4,800 places would need to be permanently removed from the 17,400 places offered by the borough's twenty-eight secondary schools. Compounding the difficulties of this massive undertaking was an unusually complicated 'dual system' into which schools had been organised when selection was abolished. Once again, too much attention had been paid to the legacy of the previous tripartite system. As a result, eight schools with six to eight forms of entry[1] for pupils between the ages of eleven and sixteen ran alongside a series of smaller linked schools catering for the eleven to fourteen and fourteen to eighteen age groups. The fall in pupil numbers threatened the larger schools with the disproportionate cost of unused places, the smaller fourteen-to-eighteen schools with a worsening in the range and level of the more academic studies for which they had been specifically established to continue and foster.

The government had recently given local authorities new powers to help them to manage their fluctuating school populations. In future, councils would be able to limit the number of pupils admitted to schools each year and so distribute demand, an astonishing reliance on institutional direction from a government supposedly committed to the workings of the invisible hand of market forces. Apart from the dubious wisdom of throwing a lifeline to underachieving schools, which could be one result, the fixed costs arising from effectively mothballing surplus accommodation not reflected in the Rate Support Grant settlement meant that even scarcer resources would be spent on empty places than on pupils; and parents were understandably furious at being denied places at schools where there was manifestly room by a government urging them to exercise greater choice. Marketeers pressed for schools to be allowed to admit to their full capacity—'open enrolment' as it was called. Such a process of natural selection, they argued, would have the benefit of driving up standards; popular schools delivering the goods would thrive, while failing schools would go to the wall. The price to be paid for this *laissez-faire* approach, however—the deleterious consequences for children trapped in declining schools—was widely and rightly judged to be too high a price to pay.

Such was the conclusion drawn by the controlling Conservative council, which was equally concerned with the need to cut unnecessary costs and improve education at the same time, in particular to take the opportunity to get rid of the dual system widely perceived to be a barely disguised continuation of the old grammar/secondary modern divide and, as such, a source of unpopular and unjustifiable inequality and unfairness. Under the energetic leadership of Peter Bowness, Croydon had established itself as a model Thatcherite council. Armed with an unassailable majority, he had enthusiastically embraced Mrs Thatcher's market agenda, opening up its services to competition in the search for value for money. Like a handful of other like-minded right-wing councils, Croydon showed 'it could be done'. Its record stood in stark contrast to the behaviour of other councils, such as Liverpool and Sheffield, where spending and trade union activity seemed alarmingly out of control and resistance to the government most entrenched. In the case of two of local government's most important organisations, the Greater London Council and the Inner London Education Authority, the conclusion was already beginning to be drawn that their outright abolition was the only answer. Peter Bowness was to play a major role in both. An admiring Margaret Thatcher rewarded him with a CBE and a knighthood within the space of six years; a peerage was to follow. With the backing of such an influential and well-connected council leader I allowed myself to believe that approval of the school reorganisation scheme I proposed, notwithstanding its extensive and radical nature, would be little more than a formality. I could not have been more mistaken.

Although the main purpose of reorganization was to reduce surplus capacity, the opportunity would be taken to replace the dual system with a uniform system based on schools catering for pupils between the ages of eleven and sixteen, each of these schools to be six forms of entry in size wherever possible. Post-sixteen education would be provided separately by means of a single Further Education tertiary college made up of five constituent centres, each serving different parts of the borough. Under these proposals, seven schools would close permanently, and most of the existing eleven-to-sixteen schools continue. The remainder, depending on their suitability in terms of condition, capacity for future development, and geographical importance, would be converted into new eleven-to-sixteen schools or into one of the four post-sixteen centres, which, along with the borough's reconstituted College of Technology, would make up the new tertiary college.

The scale and complexity of the reorganisation scheme to be presented to the government required an unusual degree of care if it were to be protected from legal challenge on procedural grounds, to which it was extensively exposed. Since and in spite of Lord Denning's *Bradford Judgment*, legal opinion had moved firmly in favour of stricter procedural observance. Detailed consultations on the minefield which lay ahead were held with DES officials. Mark Carlisle was invited to say over an informal dinner if there were anything in Croydon's plans that would cause him difficulty, a delicate matter, since, in considering the council's proposals when they formally came before him, he would need to approach them in a quasi-judicial capacity 'with clean hands' and to take into account all the representations made to him impartially. In view, however, of the radical nature of the reorganisation and the extent of the upheaval involved, it was thought no more than common sense to seek to identify any strongly held view the minister had that might cause the council to pause. As it turned out, true to his nature, Mark Carlisle had no such hang-ups, and as witness to the fact, he had taken the precaution of bringing a senior civil servant with him. No such open-mindedness, however, was shared by his influential behind-the-scenes political advisor, Stuart Sexton, who knew Croydon's education system inside out, not only as a resident, but as a former member of its education committee no less, and who had more than one axe to grind.

One of the foremost of the marketeers, Stuart had masterminded the Assisted Places Scheme whereby the government paid for selected pupils to go to independent schools. Although I did not agree with this measure, I was not unsympathetic to Stuart's broad outlook and got on well with him personally. I understood and respected the reasons for his deep distrust of comprehensive schools, rooted as they were in a personal experience I now shared. Nevertheless, he was a force to be reckoned with, and I could not count on his support. No doubt he was having his own off-the-record conversations with Mark Carlisle and with no civil servant present. In these circumstances, how would Croydon's reorganisation scheme fare?

Notwithstanding this shadowy background, plans for the future of Croydon's secondary schools to come into effect at the start of the following academic year were published on 5 June 1981 in no fewer than thirteen interlocking public notices. Under the procedures of the time, two months would be allowed for objections to be lodged. At the end of this period, any such objections would be forwarded to the secretary of state together with the council's responses.

So far so good, until 15 September, however, when everyone woke up to the shock announcement that the equable Mark Carlisle had been replaced as secretary of state by the ideologically driven Keith Joseph, who would bring an altogether different approach to bear on Croydon's proposals and be more receptive to the first-hand views of Stuart Sexton, whose services as special advisor he had retained. In spite of Sir Keith's commitment to reducing public expenditure—if there were one council responding to his call for 'cuts, cuts, cuts', it was Croydon—his prejudice against tertiary colleges proved stronger. A minute-past-midnight call from my friend at the DES told me that Croydon's scheme had been rejected. Although it fell comfortably within all the government's educational and financial policies, it had fallen foul of a single minister's strongly held personal view, the very contingency we had tried so hard to safeguard against. Months of exhaustive and unsettling work had been set at nought. 'Croydon in Baulk' shouted the headline of *The Times Educational Supplement*.

In his rejection letter Sir Keith gave his reasons. He drew attention to the disadvantageous size of four of the proposed eleven-to-sixteen schools, which the council had seen no alternative to maintaining as four forms of entry. That was fair enough, but only up to a point. Sir Keith had not sufficiently taken into account the powerful and, in our view, conclusive countervailing factors which had led the council to propose them in the first place. In any case, only one school was incapable of development beyond its present size—a single-sex school where size was less critical and which was needed in the heavily populated and built-up northern part of the borough. The offending schools, which he was later to approve, were as we all knew a smokescreen for the real reason behind his rejection of Croydon's scheme—his antagonism to the tertiary college, in particular its 'federated' management structure extending over five sites. Universities and polytechnics based on this model worked perfectly well. Sir Keith, however, took fright at its 'radical, unique, novel and untried' nature—a surprising attack from a minister more usually taking local authorities to task for their resistance to change and lack of imagination and innovation in tackling the problems of falling rolls. Sir Keith wanted to see 'large and efficient sixth forms'—this from a 'modernising' minister anguishing about deficiencies in our technical education. Unabashed, the council dug its heels in, convinced of the rightness of its approach. There was another matter. *The Guardian*'s education correspondent, David Fairhall, gave his take on the situation—'one man, one vote'. In summing up the situation so well, he had also identified a possible weakness in the secretary of state's position. Sir Keith might—just might—be on thin ice.

The discretion secretaries of state could exercise in their consideration of local education authority proposals had been heavily qualified by a recent judgment in the Court of Appeal, which had overturned a decision of the then secretary of state Fred Mulley requiring a newly elected Conservative council, Tameside, that wished to reintroduce selection, to reinstate a previous Labour-controlled council's scheme for the reorganisation of its education system along comprehensive lines. The judges ruled that the secretary of state had failed to satisfy himself that the authority was acting in a way in which no reasonable authority would have acted. This was the test the court said had to be applied; it was not for the secretary of state to substitute his view for one a local authority might reasonably hold.[2]

The point was not lost on Peter Bowness, a solicitor by profession. He led a furious delegation to a confrontation with the permanent under-secretary of state, Sir James Hamilton, flanked by the largest army of civil servants I had ever come across. Recriminations flew. In the light of the care taken on all sides in the formulation and submission of the council's proposals, how could such a debacle have arisen? The root cause, it transpired, lay in the inter-dependent nature of the council's proposals, which had not allowed the secretary of state to cherry-pick those bits he liked and reject those he did not. It was all or nothing. And no one, of course, could have anticipated such a change of minister halfway through. It was to Sir Keith that Peter Bowness next turned. It was agreed that the council would immediately resubmit proposals to close, in accordance with the original timetable, the four schools Sir Keith had previously thought too small; savings had already been factored into the education budget. These were approved within days of the expiry of the statutory notices. And it was agreed that the wider reorganisation plan would be resubmitted with face-saving modifications—three of the proposed post-sixteen centres would be established as independent, conventional sixth-form colleges under Schools Regulations. This time, the plan would go through, as it duly did in December 1982.

A New Kind of State School: The City Technology College

Normally, such a massive reorganisation would have led to a period of stability and consolidation. That had been the intention and justification of the extent of the disturbance involved. However, the appointment of yet another secretary of state, Kenneth Baker, in 1986 led to further changes of the most radical kind through the introduction of the first of a new hybrid breed of 'independent' state school, the City Technology College. The brainchild of the secretary of state himself, the CTC was a development Croydon enthusiastically supported and was anxious to include in the evolution of its education system, even at the cost of further change. Although billed as the latest of a long line of initiatives to improve Britain's lamentable technical education, which was undoubtedly one of its aims, the real purpose of the CTC was to begin the process of weakening the hegemony of local authorities and comprehensive education in earnest through two characteristics unprecedented as far as state schools were concerned. First, the CTCs would be financed directly by the government; local authorities would be bypassed altogether. Second, the comprehensive principle would be breached for the first time by admission procedures controlled by the schools themselves aimed at selecting pupils suitable for the specialised curriculum they offered through reference to 'a child's primary school record and *aptitude* as well as the attitude of parents and a long-term commitment by the family to education'—these, of all things, to be looked for in 'areas ranking high in the Environment Department's Index of Deprivation'! Other characteristics, a budget based on per capita funding, virtually complete self-management and a centrally determined curriculum were clues as to what was to come on a wider scale. Pump-priming finance was to be provided by industrial sponsors whose business outlook and input were intended to influence the make-up and direction of their colleges.

In spite of the extravagant claims for this initiative, matched by the routine apocalyptic reception by the education establishment, the CTCs failed to have any significant impact on the status and extent of technical education nationally. They were fighting decades of prejudice. Technical schools had never got off the ground. One estimate puts the number of pupils educated in them at never rising much above a pitiful 2 per cent. To create the critical mass of able, well-qualified technically educated and trained workforce, the kind to be found in Germany with which we were now regularly and enviously compared (*pace* Mrs Thatcher), Britain would have to match that country's 2000 specialist technical schools.

If the government had seriously wished to make inroads on this kind of scale into our deficiencies in this respect, all it needed was to launch a similar revolution to the comprehensive *putsch* and require each authority to provide more technical places in its area. Such a measure would not be above a secretary of state who would later take no fewer than 451 new powers to the centre and would have no compunction in telling teachers to teach standard English and multiplication tables. But that would have meant enlisting as comrade-in-arms the cooperation of local government. Anathema. As it was, the opportunity to advance technical education on the broadest front was not taken. A pity. The real and admitted aim was, of course, to undermine 'the reactionary local education authorities' and to 'shift power towards the parents and children who were the consumers of education and away from the education administrators and vested interests who were the producers of education'.[3]

The original intention was to create between twelve and twenty such 'trust schools'. In the event, fifteen were established in the five years before this phase of development came to an end. It was an uphill struggle. Sponsors and cooperative local authorities were hard to find. Kenneth Baker was fortunate in enlisting Cyril Taylor,[4] a successful entrepreneurial educationalist, to spearhead the programme. Without him the scheme would have been dead in the water. Cyril brought a welcome and much needed transatlantic energy and panache, not to say an invigorating touch of tycoonery to 'the unwieldy and complicated mechanism of raising money, interesting sponsors and keeping them enthused, and helping to find key personnel such as project managers for each CTC and the Head Teachers to develop their academic side'.[5] Kenneth Baker was right to say that without 'his enthusiasm, drive and cheerful determination, we would never have got the CTCs off the ground'. Later, on the wider front of introducing more different kinds of school into the state system, no one was to invest more personal time and effort to greater effect than Cyril Taylor.

Croydon was one of the handful of authorities approached for help with the CTC programme. Neither I nor the council had any difficulties with the concept. I had become more and more drawn to the role specialisation could play in our developing system, an attraction reinforced by my continued involvement with White Lodge. Before I left Croydon, one school, Sylvan, had been earmarked as a CTC, and talks had started along more interesting lines to establish a variant of the CTC model at Selhurst specialising in the performing arts. This was to become the BRIT School, Britain's *'Fame'* academy. The birth pangs of these two new schools illustrated all too well the difficulties in the way of breaking the mould. The Sylvan CTC proposal aroused unprecedented opposition, Labour politicians reserving for me a particularly low pit in hell. The fact of the matter was, however, as so often the case, that in spite of the sound and fury amid claims that 97 per cent of the local populace wanted to retain their 'community comprehensive', the school had attracted only forty-five pupils that year. The BRIT School could not have got off to a worse start. I had arranged to show Sir Richard Branson, a possible sponsor, round the Selhurst premises—incognito!—late one evening when it was expected we would be uninterrupted. Unfortunately, this was the evening the headmaster had decided to work late. The Labour politicians had not had long to wait for my Dantesque retribution. All hell broke loose.

Of all the government's innovations in general and Kenneth Baker's in particular, the encouragement of specialisation was to prove the most important. All the elements in the management model of the CTCs and their derivatives, the grant-maintained schools, had long been present in the independent sector. They were not revolutionary; specialisation was. By opening the way to *aptitude* taking its place alongside academic *ability*, by encouraging *pupil* as well as *parental* choice and *self*-selection in addition to *institutional* selection, such specialisation was to lead to a reinterpretation of the comprehensive principle and an unprecedented overhaul of the pattern and nature of our schools and what went on inside them.

Litigation: The Teachers Take Us to Court

All these developments, school reorganisations and the other changes that were to come, were conducted against the background of worsening relations with the teachers and an increasing tendency on both sides to resort to litigation. Between 1984 and 1987, the teachers resorted to guerrilla warfare in pursuit of better conditions and salaries. The main thrust of their strategy was to claim that many of the activities they carried out were not contractual but matters of 'goodwill', which they could withdraw as and when it suited them, making the management of the service impossible. They refused to cover for absent colleagues; left the premises during the lunch break, abandoning the supervision of school meals and midday activities; and withdrew from all meetings including those with parents held outside what they regarded as 'school time'. The advantage of 'working to rule' in this way rather than going on strike was that it allowed the teachers to be paid while wreaking havoc. This stratagem, however, did not go down well in towns where miners had been bludgeoned financially as well as physically into submission during their recent industrial disputes. Two such towns, Rotherham and Barnsley, were joined by Solihull and Croydon, middle-class boroughs at the opposite end of the social and political scale, in making token deductions by way of damages from the salaries of those teachers who, in their eyes, had broken their contracts. The NUT had no choice but to take the four authorities to the High Court.[6] They did so on what I thought their weakest ground, the previously unchallenged and time-honoured practice of teachers' standing in for absent colleagues until a supply teacher could be provided.

Mr Justice Scott did us proud, steering his judgment through no fewer than thirty-five legal precedents, not all of them immediately relevant to the untrained mind. Maritime law seemed to loom large in his thinking. The case of a drunken sailor left behind by his ship who sued successfully (!) for unpaid wages caused us some anxiety *(Button v Thompson* (1869). Eventually, after pausing at such milestones as *British Anzani (Felixstow) Ltd v International Marine Management (UK) Ltd* (1979) and *Steam Sand Pump Dredger (No 7) (owners) v Greta Holme (owners), The Greta Holme* (1897), Mr Justice Scott brought us safely into harbour and the unsurprising conclusion that teachers, unlike car plant workers paid by the hour, were professionals like doctors and solicitors, obliged to provide a service to proper professional standards not to be measured by reference to time alone. The teachers had broken their contracts, and their employing councils had been entitled to dock their wages by way of damages. One result was that we all now had a better understanding of what a teacher was obliged to do, even if this was not to the liking of the unions. The long-running and bitter dispute with the teachers was one of the 'bush fires' Sir Keith Joseph left for Kenneth Baker to put out.

The vagueness of teachers' contracts did not extend to their colleagues' in the Further Education sector, where a college's establishment was worked out by applying elaborate formulae specifying, among other things, each lecturer's duties and hours of work according to his or her relevant grade. These calculations, however, were hard to follow and open to wide interpretation. They were also open to abuse. Over time, given the colleges' gradual withdrawal from local authority scrutiny, Spanish practices had crept in, which were expensive and for which the colleges' maintaining authorities had to pay. An important element in calculations, for example, was a lecturer's 'class-contact time'. The time a lecturer actually spends in front of a class teaching might be thought to be one of the more straightforward concepts to grasp. In reality, a number of 'allowances' and 'set-offs' had imperceptibly been introduced to such an extent that additional staff not strictly necessary by the book often had to be appointed, incurring extra expense. As part of Croydon's search for savings, predictably hostile negotiations with the college lecturers' militant union, the National Association of Teachers in Further and Higher Education took place, which resulted in the council threatening all its members with dismissal if they did not accept new conditions of employment adhering more strictly to national agreements. An invitation to address an OECD conference in Australia on managing school building stock during times of fluctuating rolls could not have come at a better time. Later that year, NATFHE's close ally, the NUT chose to pick a fight over the composition of the borough's education committee.[7]

The law placed on each council which acted as an education authority a duty to establish an education committee whose views it had to take into account in discharging its functions as such. The law also required that education committees should contain 'persons of experience in education, and persons acquainted with the educational conditions prevailing in the area for which the committee acts'. Every education authority in the country, with the sole exception of Croydon, had sought to meet this requirement by co-opting teachers onto its education committee, usually on the nomination of the teachers' associations. After several vain attempts to persuade Croydon to change its mind in this matter and having equally failed to persuade the secretary of state to intervene on its behalf, the NUT, true to the litigious nature of the times and the current obsession with the membership of public bodies, took the council to court in an attempt to secure its representation on the education committee. In this, it was unsuccessful. The High Court ruled that the words 'persons of experience in education . . . were to be given their ordinary and natural meaning, which did not impart any necessity for any technical qualification as a teacher and that the phrase was properly applicable to the membership of the authority's education committee . . . It is sufficient if a person is familiar with education or has experience in the educational field'. The court was persuaded in part by the particulars of the detailed educational knowledge and experience of the great majority of the education committee members the council was able to produce.

The chairman and vice-chairman of the education committee during the main years of reorganisation and curricular reform, Derek Loughborough and David Congdon, were two such knowledgeable and experienced men. They knew the borough's education system inside out. While Derek bore the brunt of the school closures and mergers and the effects of retrenchment, David, who was later elected to Parliament, took the educational debate about resources, numbers and quantity onto the much more substantive and difficult ground of purpose and quality, of teaching and learning and the curriculum which had been moving up the national agenda, albeit slowly, since Mr Callaghan's Ruskin College speech.

The Curriculum

When I was a history teacher, it was left to me to decide what history should be taught, which was not difficult, as I had strong and clear views on the subject and I still had my notes from university. The only outside influences I had to take into account were the requirements of the examination boards and the views of the head of the history department, whose job it naturally was to see that her team presented a coherent front. No one else had any involvement in what went on in my classroom, and no one showed any interest. That was the way it was throughout the country and, it was widely held, had always been. But this was far from the case.

From the outset, the introduction of the national education system had been accompanied by Codes and Regulations laid down by the government, stipulating in some detail what was to be taught in its elementary and secondary schools, forming in effect a national curriculum. Over the years, these Codes and Regulations had been reviewed and, each time, relaxed. *The Elementary Code* was discontinued in 1927, when it was replaced by a *Handbook of Suggestions for Teachers*, the title graphically showing the way things were going. The Regulations for Secondary Schools, however, survived until the 1944 Act, whereupon the curriculum as a national concern effectively disappeared from view. In spite of this, there was a large measure of unspoken assumption and agreement about the body of knowledge to be conveyed. 'Tell the children that Wolfe won Quebec' (not, of course, 'by instruction or order but by suggestion') was the only injunction Churchill laid on R.A. Butler when he appointed him President of the Board of Education in 1941. On 7 February 1946, I was writing in my primary school exercise book, which I still have, 'Quebec was built on a rocky hill, below which a great river ran. The French general ordered soldiers to guard the city.' I doubt whether there had been any ministerial communication with Miss Pritchard.

The only subject specified to be taught in the nation's schools according to the 1944 Act was the one usually forbidden in most other countries, namely religious education, which seemed during the Act's passage through Parliament to take up most of the members' time. The Act had nothing to say about the rest of the curriculum or secular instruction as it was then tellingly called, except how responsibility for it was to be distributed. I give below Mr Butler's description of this division, which was carried into legislation, because of its importance as the background to the changes which were to come and because of the surprising, in retrospect, prominence he gave to specialisation.

> I propose to give, so far as I can, a definition, which we have in mind at present, subject to future negotiation, of the various bounds of responsibility (for the ordinary secular instruction of the pupil) of the local education authority, the governing body and the head teacher . . . Taking the three bodies . . . who will control this matter, the local authority, the governing body and the head teacher, I will begin by saying that the local education authority, as I see it, will have responsibility for the broad type of education given in the secondary schools, including the aided grammar schools and other aided secondary schools, and its place in the local system according to the local needs. The broad picture will be governed, so far as I can foresee the future, by the needs of the district and the

needs of the children. To develop that point, I would say that I imagine that, if it appeared to the authority that a certain school was particularly good in the higher ranges of scientific or mathematical study, they might agree to a tendency for that school to specialise in that direction, while other schools might specialise in different directions. The governing body would, in our view, have the general direction of the curriculum as actually given from day to day within the school. The head teacher would have, again in our view, responsibility for the internal organization of the school, including the discipline that is necessary to keep the pupils applied to their study, and to carry out the curriculum in the sense desired by the governing body.

In spite of the fact that local councils controlled a majority of the members of governing bodies at that time, none ever sought to involve itself in the curriculum. In practice, responsibility for what children were taught was delegated or, more to the point, left to the teachers themselves. Ronald Gould, the general secretary of the NUT, well summed up the mentality of the times: 'I have heard it said that the existence in this country of 146 strong, vigorous local education authorities safeguards democracy and lessens the risk of dictatorship. No doubt this is true, but an even greater safeguard is the existence of a quarter of a million teachers who are free to decide what should be taught and how it should be taught.' In other words the curriculum was little more than what each and every teacher was minded to impart.

Such was the position which remained unchallenged until Mr Callaghan's intervention. After his clear prime-ministerial pointer towards the need for and desirability of reforms to the curriculum and assessment, it might have been thought that his own government would have made progress on both fronts. Not a bit of it. An indication of the foot-dragging which was about to characterise the Labour government's approach to reform during its remaining time in office may be seen in the lacklustre title of the Green Paper intended to follow up Mr Callaghan's initiative, *Education in Schools*, a poor contrast in title and contents to *A Nation at Risk: the Imperative for Legislation*, Bill Bennett's splendid publication grappling with the same issues in the United States.[8] That was more like it.

Britain's Green Paper revealed no such similar sense of urgency. It was 'sparse in content and complacent in tone'.[9] The threefold division of responsibility for the management of schools was uncritically endorsed. Local education authorities would be asked to 'review' their 'curricular arrangements', after which the government would issue 'advice'. Whether there should be a 'core curriculum' would be 'examined'. On the matter of performance, the subjective and qualitative nature of inspections was endorsed: '*Schools should assess their performance against their own objectives*'(my italics). It was surprising that pupils were not allowed to mark their own examination papers. Anything of a concrete nature was dismissed in concrete terms: 'It has been suggested that individual pupils should, at certain ages, take external tests of basic literacy and numeracy of national character and universally applied . . . The Secretaries of State reject this view . . . ' And so on. In Nicholas Timmins' words, 'The Green Paper itself proposed little more than consultations about a review which would lead to consultations about the advice that the department might issue on the subject'—a truly lamentable state of affairs.

Stories of the government's impotence abounded and were even regaled with a sense of pride. Fred Mulley, the secretary of state to whom James Callaghan entrusted his reform programme, boastfully complained that the only power he had was to demolish unused air raid shelters in school playgrounds. The DES, it was said, had the engine of a lawnmower and the brakes of an army tank. Bernard Donoughue, Callaghan's advisor, who had prompted the prime minister's intervention, was scathing. In his view, the Green Paper was the product of 'Whitehall at its self-satisfied, condescending and unimaginable worst' and 'the resistance of professional vested interests to radical change'.

During the nine years between Shirley Williams' Green Paper in 1977 and Kenneth Baker's appointment as secretary of state in 1986, nothing effectively was done to grasp the nettles of curricular and assessment reform. In the hands of the public school *philosophes* at the DES who were clearly in the driving seat, both issues became overly academic exercises. Lack of progress was laid at the door of the department's most powerful official, its deputy secretary, Walter Ulrich, who had set his face against any substantive change to the status quo. Accounts of meetings at the DES during these years describe them—often in my view with a misplaced sense of superiority of how we do things in this country—as akin to postgraduate seminars. The arrival of Sir Keith Joseph at the department, an intellectual in his own right if ever there was one, did nothing to change the situation in spite of his sincerely and strongly held view that deficiencies in the education system were a major cause of Britain's economic decline, and in spite of the fact that he truly wanted to do something about this, including, through reforming the curriculum, aligning the work of schools more with the world of work. Too often, one minister felt, the secretary of state 'would end up admiring Walter's fine Wykehamist mind and concede the intellectual point rather than persist with the political argument'.[10]

Sir Robert Morant, another Wykehamist, is often traduced for embedding the class distinctions and assumptions of his time in the country's national curriculum and failing to use the powers of the state to create a mass education system equal to the needs of the age. The same might be said of his privileged successors. In frustrating curricular reform—and the voucher—the DES would withhold from the country at large the benefits of the public school education many of its officials had themselves enjoyed. The means whereby the state schools could become more like the public schools—the aim of Margaret Thatcher and Sir Keith Joseph—were not to be countenanced; *une trahison des clercs* of a pretty tall order.

At his first, celebrated, meeting with his civil servants, Sir Keith had given them to read Max Wilkinson's thorough and trenchant *Lessons from Europe: a Comparison of British and West European Schooling*, which had identified lack of central direction as a main weakness in Britain's education system. As with vouchers, Sir Keith may have been attracted by its arguments, but he was going to act on his instincts. 'God forbid that any English Minister of Education should ever make any subject compulsory . . . except religious observance of course'(!) Others felt less constrained. In the face of mounting economic difficulties and evidence of contributing educational failure—of 915,000 pupils who left school in 1979, 434,000 did so with only one GCE O Level, a fact Sir Keith himself was fond of quoting—David Young, the secretary of state for employment, joined with Kenneth Baker, the minister for technical information, to construct a well-defined programme of vocational and technical courses for the fourteen-to-nineteen age group. The Technical and Vocational Education Initiative, financed separately by the Department for Employment, was in both these respects a forerunner of things to come.

The specific nature of the TVEI courses contrasted strongly with the welter of confusing, overlapping and often conflicting publications[11] emanating from the DES and HM Inspectorate of Schools between 1979 and 1986 giving the 'government's 'recommended'—albeit far from certain—'approach' to be used as reference by local education authorities in the review of their curricular policies requested by the 1977 Green Paper: on the one hand the DES championed a 'core' curriculum, on the other HM Inspectorate argued for a 'common' curriculum. Within its existing statutory framework, which would remain unchanged, the curriculum was described in the most general, abstract terms. It should be 'broad', 'balanced', 'differentiated', and 'relevant'. Its aims were 'to help pupils to develop lively, enquiring minds, the ability to question and argue rationally and to apply themselves to tasks and physical skills', 'to help pupils to use language and number'. Subjects, we were warned, were 'a kind of shorthand whose real educational meaning depends on *the school's definition of what it expects children will learn and be able to do*' (my italics).

Alternatively, the curriculum could be seen as areas of 'understanding and experience' such as 'the aesthetic and creative, ethical, linguistic . . .' or as 'skills required at particular ages'. Impelled by the government's obsessive determination to avoid anything that could be regarded as content or 'detail', we waded through a thicket of 'elements', 'constituents', and 'propositions'. The legislators of the time gave more attention to the composition of governing bodies than to the curriculum—I never understood how putting the caretaker on the governing body of a school or college was intended to improve the education it offered; I was sure that having a clear idea of what pupils should be learning would. References to 'grammar' and 'arithmetic' were studiously avoided. The word 'syllabus' was mentioned rarely and then only to be dismissed: 'Neither government nor the local education authority should specify in detail what schools should teach'. In spite of the undoubted formidable intellect and industry the DES invested in its deliberations and resulting documents, its efforts came under heavy criticism. Its resulting booklet

The School Curriculum (1981) was described as: 'A confused document lacking in intellectual distinction and practicality alike. Many have doubted the DES's competence in the area of the curriculum and this document will do nothing to dispel these doubts.'[12]

In terms of *content*, the Department of Education and Science had chosen to put the narrowest construction on the definition of the word 'curriculum' and the broadest on education as *process*. In so doing, it deprived itself and local government—on which alone a duty of efficiency lay and which it was repeatedly called upon to discharge—an indispensable management tool. It is hard to imagine how central government itself could hope to manage one of its own main responsibilities, teacher supply, which was in an admittedly chaotic state, without having a reliable idea of what schools were expected to teach. Max Wilkinson might as well have pinpointed lack of content in addition to central control as one of the reasons for the inadequacies of our much complained about education system. The government's documents made a sort of sense within the profession, but for local politicians and parents trying to find out what was being taught in schools they were useless. Take my own subject, history, for example.

The Lesson of History

> English government has a special claim to be studied. It developed in comparative freedom from outside interference, producing a curious blend of decentralized and popular freedom with strong, efficient and centralized administration. Of these two ingredients neither ought to be ignored, though the first has always struck observers as the more important. In truth, English history has been as remarkable for good government as for free and constitutional government, though the two have not always coincided . . .

This straightforward view of history with which my tutor, Geoffrey Elton, opens his most important work, *The Tudor Revolution in Government*, was not shared by officials at the DES, although I imagine that most who had a deciding say in the matter would have been taught along these lines. According to the department, the purpose of history was to introduce pupils to such 'concepts' as 'chronology and cause and effect' and the 'weighing of evidence from different sources, opportunity to become acquainted with written material of different types and to learn to distinguish fact from fiction'. Few if any would quarrel with these lofty sentiments. But how did all this work out in practice? Looking through my sons' schoolwork in Richmond, I found that the history they were learning bore absolutely no relation to the history I had learned at school and university, which had taken me through the familiar timeline of the great events and people that had shaped our island story. 'Have we ever had a dictator in this country?' my fourteen-year-old son asked. 'Oliver Cromwell,' I ventured. 'Never heard of him.'

Indeed, history as a subject had, like the Lord Protector, disappeared altogether, in many cases swallowed up into something called Humanities. Extraordinarily, children who were considered unable to handle facts were instead invited to empathize with people living in times past and their conditions, a faculty which did not seem to fit into Piaget's theories of child development, elsewhere underpinning much of the progressive educationalists' agenda.

> The way to involve your pupils imaginatively in the lives of Elizabethan people would be, after preparation, to take them to see an English manor-house like Charlecote . . . With some preparation we could recreate in our pupils' imagination the scene in Charlecote's great day when Queen Elizabeth called. The men in the brewhouse would have been working into the night. The women would have been working overtime laundering white cloth. Then would come the news that Elizabeth had left Kenilworth. Sir Thomas Lucy would have a last look round, seeing that the boy had driven the fallow deer to be near at hand in the great park, sipping the wine, curling his moustache. The musicians would do a final quiet tuning up in the gallery of the banqueting hall. Today in the hall there is a figure of the Queen made from a death mask. It is a sharp face and there is a slight curl to the lip. What words came from these lips during the meal? Was everything very formal and flowery and complimentary, or did the Queen let her hair down?[13]

As content was subordinated to process in this way, it did not matter what body of knowledge, assuming it could be described as such, was used for the purpose of engaging the pupils' interest. I could not understand why it was not possible to marry the government's, and by extension the teachers', often qualitative view of history with a knowledge of the facts which had turned the past into the present. Could not a pupil be introduced to the concept of cause and effect by learning about the inventions of Arkwright and Hargreaves and their impact on the Industrial Revolution? Indeed, would not such a concept be more easily and effectively conveyed in this manner? It seemed to me that teachers would find their work more manageable and acceptable to parents if they taught their subjects more and their pupils less. As it was, the absence of content and aims from the curriculum left teaching open to every form of practice, which could be and was used to mask pupil failure and deflect public disappointment and criticism. The way I had progressed through my history studies had, to me at least, shown how false and artificial the claimed antithesis between content and process was. 'Give an account of the fall of the Roman Empire' at GCE O Level had given way at A Level to 'Account for the fall of the Roman Empire'. By the time I had reached the Cambridge Entrance Examination, the question had become 'How far did the Roman Empire fall?' or something similar.

Gone, too, along with anything I could recognise as history, was the discipline of the timed essay, replaced by open-ended 'topics' to be worked on whenever my children thought fit, introducing them to a sense of time, or rather timelessness, they could have well done without at that stage in their lives. The government would have them leave school without knowledge of or even a nodding acquaintanceship with Magna Carta, the Acts of Supremacy and of Settlement, the Bill of Rights, and so forth, and they did. They would not have done so had they gone to Winchester or even Cheltenham College for that matter. If only they had Mr Stewart as their teacher.

> MR STEWART. Well, if you insist on staring at me like a lot of
> Christmas puddings, you can at least write. Perhaps you'll
> allow me to teach you, Travis, to make drudgery divine. It
> has been said . . .

> TRAVIS *stands by the window and leans against the wall to pull his trouser bottoms out of his socks.*

> MR STEWART, *continuing.* Of George the Third, he was a mollusc who never found his rock. *His gaze settles on Travis.*

> TRAVIS. Plumb, J. H. Plumb.

> MR STEWART, *his eyes glazing a moment.* Possibly. What were the failures (*he walks towards his desk*) of the British Constitution and the political parties that prevented the mollusc king from finding his rock? A twenty minute essay without notes. (*He sits down and tilts back his chair, puts his feet up on the desk, and takes the* Daily Express *out of his pocket.*)

> DENSON, *whispering.* What's a mollusc, for God's sake?[14]

Piaget could have told him.[15]

For such personal, as well as professional, reasons, I had long been persuaded that the curriculum should belong to a wider responsibility than the schools and teachers themselves—if not the local authority then preferably the government itself—and had begun to campaign through articles and speeches for the adoption of a national curriculum, for which there was next to no support. Both the left-wing education establishment and the right-wing market reformers were against it, as were the prime minister and the secretary of state in the most emphatic terms. When Mrs Thatcher routinely referred me to Sir Keith, usually accompanied by a warning about 'what the Germans had done to their curriculum', she would have known only too well what kind of reception I would get.

THE CROYDON CURRICULUM

I knew only too well what the Germans had done to their curriculum. The German School in Richmond where the children of German citizens living in London are able to follow the same curriculum they would follow in their own country was only a stone's throw from the school my sons attended, enabling me to compare and contrast their school day with that of their continental counterparts at first hand. If Goethe and Bismarck could be met head on, why not Shakespeare and Henry V?

Opponents of a prescribed curriculum advanced two basic arguments. First, learning arises essentially from the interaction between pupil and teacher, in which nothing should be allowed to intervene. Second, the means of any such attempted intervention is open to abuse, indoctrination being the most commonly cited. As far as the pupil-teacher relationship was concerned, no one was seeking to interfere with how teachers taught; this was and is unquestionably the *sine qua non* of effective learning. In any case, no written instruction, however intrusive, could realistically expect to affect the intimate chemistry of learning; and public policy towards education as a whole could not be expected to rest on any one such aspect, however significant. Many people, if not most, will be indebted to one or more outstanding teachers, but not all their teachers all the time. I know only too well how much I owe my history teacher, Eric Green, and many others. I also know how often I was badly taught.

Any indiscriminate appeal to 'the pupil-teacher relationship' as something single, settled, and universally and unfailingly successful was shot to pieces, in my eyes, by what went on in the workplace, for which I bore a responsibility. Not everyone was being taught by Robert Donat or Maggie Smith.[16] Nearer to reality was the experience of a pupil in one of Croydon's schools who had passed through the hands of no fewer than nineteen different mathematics teachers in one year. The high rates of teacher wastage and turnover compounded the effects of the fragmentation caused by the teachers' control over what they taught. Subject matter was duplicated or omitted altogether. The dinosaurs were done three times, but we never seemed to get beyond the Industrial Revolution. I had taken up my history place at Cambridge in the fond expectation that I would at last do so, only to discover that, as far as the university was concerned, modern history began with fifth-century Athens! I would have to start all over again. Beneath the high-flown rhetoric, the curriculum was an unholy mess.

To the argument that public and lay control of the curriculum was open to abuse, my reply was that I would prefer to have the content of lessons decided in open debate than behind closed classroom doors. Stuart Sexton, an arch-opponent of my centralising tendencies in this respect, complained to me about a lesson drawn to his attention in which the use of a contraceptive had been demonstrated by its being placed over a test tube. What would he prefer? To leave sex education to the vagaries of the individual teacher or formulated in a way whereby everyone would know what was to be expected? I saw my role as being involved in the latter, rather than fielding councillors' questions about caretakers' overtime, the cost of hiring a piano, or why a school's lights had been left on in the evening. I for one had no compunction in letting them into the secret garden.

In responding to the government's request that it review its curricular arrangements,[17] Croydon, alone of education authorities in the country, took the opportunity of the loophole so offered to assume responsibility for what was taught in its schools. The council sought to lay down what that should be, inviting its teachers to see the curriculum not as a prescription on them but as an entitlement guaranteeing all children the knowledge, understanding and skills we could together agree they would need to fulfil themselves as individuals, to earn their living and to take their place in society. The extensive consultation exercise which followed was led and managed by specialist inspectors and advisors and teachers who had made a reputation for themselves in their subjects. In spite of the fractious relationship that existed between the council and the profession over reorganisation, cuts, privatisation and conditions of service, hundreds of teachers took part in what turned out to be a constructive, good-natured, level-headed collaborative effort.

Once the ritual opening shots had been fired, there was little antagonism. The willingness among local teachers to share their thoughts, which contrasted with the sulky stand-off by their national unions, arose from a growing awareness of the need to engage parents realistically in their

children's education—places on the governing body were not enough—
and to secure the support of the public in their campaign for better
conditions and salaries. Many were also concerned about making sure
that their subject areas did not lose out in what was now seen as an
inevitable process of definition. Sir Keith Joseph had loudly and darkly
complained about 'clutter'. It was clear early on that the curriculum
would be overburdened and that priorities would need to be set, the local
task which awaited me at the end of the consultative period. It fell to me
to try to make sense of it all.

Characteristically, R.A. Butler had anticipated the situation I found
myself in. In introducing his Bill, he had drawn attention to 'the danger
that the Secretary (later the Secretary of State) or Director of Education
may fancy himself in certain subjects or in some branch of study and
by an *obiter dictum* try to direct the secular instruction of that school
as he would say, according to the wishes of the Authority'. And he
had guarded against it: 'In future, major changes to the curriculum
should be brought formally before the Local Education Authority and
the Governors; and not in some chance way'. Not everything in the
mountain of paper that confronted me was to my liking. I was particularly
disappointed that the English and the history curricula were not more
factually detailed. I had to settle for the aim that pupils leaving school
in Croydon would 'have sufficient knowledge and understanding of
British History including the Modern Period to be able to comment
sensibly on the historical dimension of national events, and to be aware
of the cultural, political and social heritage we possess'. This fell far
short of what I wished to achieve. Nevertheless, I would have to stick
to what was before me.

The paper produced for public consultation, the next stage, received a
warm welcome in the borough, most helpfully from *The Croydon Advertiser*,
whose editor, Geoff Collard, was an enthusiast for a written curriculum
and the council's efforts. He chaired one of the public meetings. It was
not all plain sailing. At a time of cutbacks, some parents saw the exercise
as a cynical smokescreen, as 'pie in the sky'. 'You say that every child
should have the opportunity to play a musical instrument. My child hasn't
because there are not enough instruments to go round at his school,'
complained one parent. Geoff Collard's reply that, without the statement

of policy the council had sent him, the parent would not have been able to ask the question, was music to my ears. The paper, *'The Curriculum: Towards a Common Approach: A Statement of Policy'* was approved by the council in July 1984 after one of the most statesmanlike of debates with only one unsuccessful attempt by Labour members to amend it in one detail. Forty thousand copies of Croydon's curriculum statement *What Every Child Should Know* were distributed throughout the borough. The inevitable accusations of extravagance were more than adequately met by the response of one parent, 'No one has ever thought that this was something which should involve me'.

In most respects, the Croydon Curriculum was a scissors and paste affair, freely acknowledging its reliance on the background papers the DES and HM Inspectorate had prepared over the years, and other learned publications; the Bullock Report on the teaching of English and the Cockroft Report on the teaching of mathematics, for example. It could make no claim to originality as far as content was concerned. Its significance lay: first, in its legal status—in future what children were taught in Croydon would be decided democratically by society at large; second, the fact that it would be implemented—the time for talk and discussion was over; and third, the degree of detail and specificity with which it treated key issues—the ground to be covered. An attempt was made to formulate aims to be reached in all subjects at certain stages and to identify the levels of attainment in English and mathematics expected at ages seven, eleven and fourteen. It was agreed as matters of policy that standardised tests should be used in these two subjects, that, generally, classes should be organised according to pupils' ability, and that arrangements should be made whereby pupils should be able to progress not automatically by reference to their age but according to the stages of attainment they had reached—the subject of the Labour members' objection.

Crucially, the Croydon Curriculum received a broad welcome in the national media as well as the local press, from *The Financial Times* to *The Guardian. The Evening Standard* gave influential support. The extent and flavour of the coverage we were getting was not lost on Bernard Ingham, Margaret Thatcher's Press Officer, who lived in Croydon and had a ringside seat. In the morning, I found myself arguing with Ted Wragg[18] on the BBC's Radio *Today Programme*. In the evening, I was on television being propped up against ITN's Big Ben background announcing to my startled family and the nation, amid *News at Ten*'s introductory chimes: *Bong*, 'In future, children will go through school according to how well they are doing and not how old they are.' *Bong*.

But what would Sir Keith think? My friend at headquarters rang to say that he had been with the secretary of state that morning as he ticked his way through Croydon's paper to such warm words of approval that he thought he should telephone to relay Sir Keith's opinion, not quite 'Why can't all local authorities be like Croydon?' but near enough. Sir Keith's private approbation was, however, not to be carried into public policy. He came to a conference on the curriculum held by the council to tell us so in person, although we were making headway of sorts. Sir Keith said he didn't like 'over-centralised control'. But there was, he conceded, a need to 'arrive at a nationally agreed view of objectives and define in a better way the content of the curriculum. Without clear objectives it would be impossible to assess the performance of the education system and teachers would be unable to ensure coherence and continuity in their work.'

Notwithstanding Sir Keith's personal views, Croydon had put the government on the spot. The decision the DES had so successfully sought to obscure, delay and prevent for almost ten years—who should decide what the nation's children should learn and their teachers teach—could no longer be postponed. Unwilling to assume responsibility for the curriculum itself, there was no chance the government would entrust the curriculum to 'Loony Left' councils such as Lambeth and Islington, already being pencilled in as possible future education authorities. What if they, following Croydon's example, took control of the curriculum and came up with their own ideas? Would they not prefer to deal with racism, disarmament, peace studies, women's rights, gender and other issues of the day, to their way of thinking 'more relevant' than the recognisable approach sketched out by Croydon and official opinion? But as Emily Blatch[19] put it, 'We cannot legislate for our friends'. Things could not, however, remain as they were, and support for a national curriculum was at last beginning to make headway. In April 1986, Lord Beloff[20] moved an amendment to the latest education bill requiring responsibility for the curriculum to be exercised 'in accordance with the priorities that the secretary of state may have from time to time.'

In so doing he referred to a letter I had written to *The Times*.[21] 'It is sometimes quite fairly argued against my occasional contributions to our debates on education that my own experience of the state system is limited and that I am speaking from a theoretical point of view. I should like, therefore, to pray in aid a letter which my noble lords may have read. It appeared in The Times newspaper of 12 April—not very long ago. As it is a long letter, I shall read only one paragraph. It says, 'The government representing the widest interests of society should accept a more open and direct responsibility for what is taught in schools and for its cost and unite the service behind a national curriculum in tune with the needs of the country as a whole.' That letter did not come from a theoretician. It was signed by Donald Naismith, the director of education for the London Borough of Croydon.'

Condemned as an 'extraordinarily revolutionary proposal',[22] Lord Beloff's amendment was soundly defeated, and a thoroughly confused government went on to give in the resulting Act[23] 'the determination and organisation of the secular curriculum to the headteacher'. Although a desperate piece of improvisation which could not last, astonishment greeted Kenneth Baker's announcement within a year of his appointment as secretary of state of his support for a national curriculum.

The National Curriculum

This *volte-face* in government policy is not easy to explain, in spite of the problems caused by the resurgence of local authority assertiveness in curricular matters. In his first major speech as education secretary, Kenneth Baker had told the House of Commons: 'We operate though a decentralized school system, and I believe in such diffusion of power. It is right to devolve responsibility even in a national service like education. I have been asked frequently whether I favour adopting the French centralized system. I want to make it clear that I do not.' Seven months later, I was met at the door of Number 10 by Bernard Ingham to tell me that lunch was off but that it was now unnecessary as I 'had got my national curriculum'. The lady had been for turning, on this issue at least. Official accounts, including the autobiographies of Kenneth Baker and Margaret Thatcher, shed no light on their Damascene conversion.

My own view is this. Beneath Sir Keith's protracted indecisiveness and his department's vapourings about the curriculum, right-wing marketeers within government circles were making headway. They were spearheaded by Stuart Sexton and 'back to basics' ministers such as Bob Dunn and Rhodes Boyson, together with pressure groups outside government such as the Hillgate Group and the Centre for Policy Studies, led by the redoubtable Sheila Lawlor. They lobbied hard for a return to selection, vouchers, opting out, school-based management, the ending of academic tenure, open enrolment, and formula funding—anything to break the stranglehold of local education authorities and the comprehensive school monopoly. *Whose Schools?* the title of a publication of the Hillgate Group in 1986 summed up their manifesto. Their difficulty was that each of their proposals, piecemeal, not only entailed considerable political and practical difficulties but lacked the unifying strategy only a national curriculum could provide to legitimise and bring about the institutional changes sought. And to any such government involvement in the curriculum they were resolutely opposed. Of the ministers involved only Chris Patten,[24] to my knowledge, saw that a demand-led system would, paradoxically, need to be underpinned by a national curriculum, without which the mechanisms to liberate schools from local government control could not be supported intellectually nor put into effective practice if the government were to fulfil its national responsibilities.

The marketeers, on the other hand wanted to roll back the state in every respect. They did not want the state to be rolling back, most definitely not one in which the education secretary could 'decide what is history and how the apostrophe should be used'.[25] And they certainly were not in favour of the local authority having anything to do with the curriculum. But what about the schools and the teachers themselves? How far could they be trusted? Many of the marketeers held the naive and sentimental view that, free from local authority control, comprehensives would transform themselves overnight into Highbury Groves and St Joseph's Colleges,[26] a view not widely shared. As the treatment of homosexuality in school lessons had already demonstrated, recourse to the government itself was often the only way their values stood a chance of survival.[27]

Margaret Thatcher would realise her atomised vision of a local education authority-free system of largely independent schools able to select their intakes and even charge fees, themes she returned to again and again to the despair of her ministers, only if the state were able to safeguard and pursue its own considerable legitimate interests in what and how well its future citizens were taught. Without a coherent, shared programme of learning and standardised methods of assessing the performance of pupils and schools, it was impossible to see how equality of opportunity and social justice, along with transparency and accountability, could be secured; how resources could be sensibly planned and monitored; and how the education and training of a constantly changing workforce could be kept up to date.

The national curriculum introduced by the enactment of Kenneth Baker's Great Reform Bill was, therefore, the necessary precondition of the other changes the Bill contained aimed at advancing the market agenda, which had been extensively trailed over the past decade or more. The true import of the legislation would have been more honestly expressed if these anti-local authority measures had preceded the provisions of the national curriculum, which were given pride of place. Nevertheless, at long last, the basic building blocks of a demand-led education system were being wheeled into place. All schools were given wider powers over expenditure, pupil recruitment and the appointment of staff; those schools whose parents so wished could opt out of local authority control altogether to become grant-maintained, financed directly by the government through formula-funding, linking the amount spent to the numbers on roll—the nearest we were going to get to vouchers; City Technology Colleges were officially launched. And as if all this were not enough, tacked onto the Bill as an afterthought, the result of an amendment, the Inner London Education Authority, the country's most significant education authority, was to be abolished. Just like that.

The Abolition of the Inner London Education Authority

I viewed the abolition of ILEA with mixed feelings. Although I had not become one of London's teachers out of any sense of idealism, I nevertheless shared the strong sense of mission which ran through everything its education authority did and had felt part of its fight with the formidable problems of the inner city. But I had also experienced its shortcomings as a large monopoly provider with an unyielding mindset towards the nature and pattern of the education it wished to provide. Although achieving lower costs was certainly one of the reasons Thatcherite marketeers sought to break up local government services and the public utilities, it was not their only motive. Marketeers also hoped to open them up to new ways of thinking and doing things, against which local government all too often launched the kind of lumpen resistance County Hall[28] had mounted against the outdoor pursuits centre for youngsters from south-east London I had set up at Inverliever in the Western Highlands as a teacher with ILEA's predecessor, the LCC.

The centre's purpose was to offer a wide range of leisure activities, cultural as well as sporting, to young people, principally those who did not benefit from the conventional youth services because they found it hard to 'join in' or did not want to 'sign up'—'unattached youth' as they were beginning to be called. Based on the Highlands centre being established by the maverick Scottish headmaster, R.F. McKenzie, at Inverlair, Inverliever ran into the same kind of opposition from the education establishment and succeeded only through the generosity of the great charitable foundations and the determination and energy of local volunteers, whose can-do spirit contrasted sharply with the uninterested obfuscation of the official bodies we had to deal with and which should have been on our side.

In spite of its public support for Inverliever, the government took refuge in the regulations governing grants to the youth service, which restricted expenditure of public money to schemes in England and Wales; perversely and predictably, the secretary of state for Scotland was empowered to spend money in England. And although enthusiastically backed by the local council, Greenwich, not then an education authority, County Hall refused practical help on the grounds that, if it supported Inverliever, it would have to support other similar projects, a depressing, egalitarian argument of the worst kind and a powerful brake on innovation. Given the nature of the times, lack of money was a fair enough reason, but it was hard to avoid the impression that schools were not meant to strike out in these kinds of ways on their own and that experimentation and innovation were properly and exclusively the province of the authority.

ILEA was the direct descendant of the London School Board, founded in 1870 to treat the capital city as a single entity for the purpose of providing an education service. From many points of view and for many years, this made eminently good sense. Although abolition of ILEA has been variously portrayed as 'disgraceful', 'malicious', a 'stitch-up', and a 'noxious example of political spite',[29] few now believe that its breakup was the 'massive act of vandalism' claimed.[30] Leaving aside the usual litany of criticism—size, expense, ideology and performance—the reason it had to go, *au fond*, was that it had shown itself incapable of responding to a changing society, in particular one in which parents were beginning to demand a greater and more realistic say in the kind of education they wished for their children.

The duty I personally found most difficult and disagreeable as education officer was to administer the admission of pupils to schools, to 'allocate' places as the terminology bleakly put it. Too often, this meant directing pupils, against the wishes of their parents, to schools to which they did not want to go and denying them places in schools which could clearly accommodate them but which were administratively 'full'. The law laid on parents the duty of educating their children. It did not, in my view, provide them with anything like the means to make this obligation meaningful. There were simply not enough places of sufficient variety to reflect the differing needs of children. Nor were there methods of administration available whereby parents could control the decisions they wished to take. Over the years, I had become persuaded that diversity of genuine choice for pupils as well as parents should be a prime policy aim. The launching of London's inner boroughs as new education authorities in place of ILEA offered the prospect of a fresh start.

The abolition of ILEA shared many of the characteristics of the government's eventual acceptance of a national curriculum; years of indecision, drift and delay in the face of practical difficulties until a local government intervention showed the way forward, this time in the shape of a coterie of three uncompromising right-wing Conservative boroughs, Westminster, Kensington and Chelsea, and Wandsworth, arguing that they and perhaps other inner boroughs should take over education in their areas. Although ILEA's break-up had first surfaced as a serious policy option nationally in 1980, it had already made its appearance in Wandsworth soon after the Conservatives' local election victory there two years earlier. During the election campaign, Paul Beresford,[31] who was eventually to become council leader, had been made forcibly aware on the doorstep of public dissatisfaction with ILEA's shortcomings, which he himself had already experienced as a parent. Recently arrived from New Zealand, he was dismayed at the quality of education in the borough which contrasted poorly with the schooling his family had left behind. From the outset of their administration, therefore, Wandsworth's Conservatives had placed the abolition of ILEA and the dispersal of its responsibilities among the inner boroughs alongside their wide-ranging programme of privatising council services which was quickly to enter government policy as, in time, their approach to education in the capital was to do.

As solutions to the problems posed by the replacement of ILEA were discarded one after the other—the delegation of its responsibilities to the constituent boroughs by no means the only possible solution—Paul Beresford's lobbying on behalf of Westminster, Kensington and Chelsea, and Wandsworth in the end paid off, their political arguments reinforced by proven track records of managerial achievement assuaging many of the practical concerns which had stood in the way. There was another reason. During Paul Beresford's campaign in Wandsworth, he had made no secret of his determination, once in control of education locally, to enable the borough's schools to run themselves on independent lines, an idea which in public aroused apoplectic hostility but which in private conversation with the prime minister met with enthusiastic approval. His party's liberalising policies counterbalanced by tight financial control were transforming the run-down part of London it had inherited; it would similarly transform education. If there was a place and time to replace Sir Keith's 'compulsory, coerced, conscripted' education system, it was here and it was now.

CHAPTER FOUR

WANDSWORTH 1988-1994

Until recently the prevailing pattern of secondary education in Wandsworth—as in most parts of the country—was based on the neighbourhood comprehensive school. The idea was that such schools would cater fully for the varying needs of all the children in their locality.

I believe that this concept is mistaken educationally, and has been convincingly proved to be so over the past 30 years. I also believe it wrong that most parents should have little else to choose from than from a virtual monopoly of one kind of school. Parents, in my view, have a right to exercise real choice from a range of genuinely different schools which reflects their wishes and needs and those of their children.

Diversity and Choice, A Consultative Document, September 1992
Foreword by the Leader of the Council,
Councillor Edward Lister[1]

Municipal Conservatism: 'The Wandsworth Way'

Eddie Lister, chairman of the education planning committee, appointed to set up the new authority, and Sir Paul Beresford, the leader of the council, had waited a long time to take over education from ILEA. Now with the decision to let all the inner boroughs manage education in their area, they could hardly conceal their impatience, but they would have to wait a little longer. Nothing of practical effect could be decided until the formal handover on 31 March 1990, when, agonisingly, they might be nearing the end of their time in office. Who could say? In the local elections due that year, they would be defending a majority of one, a cliffhanging situation which had lent their advertisement for an education officer a certain vertiginous attraction.

In any case, much of the two-year run-up period would be spent designing and recruiting a new education department from scratch and transferring to the new authority its share of the physical apparatus of ILEA, its property and personnel, both massive undertakings in themselves but made easier by Wandsworth's impressively efficient administrative machine. For once, I was grateful for corporate management. More importantly, these two years provided invaluable time during which to confront the more difficult task of hammering out the detailed policies needed to meet the majority party's clear but less specific aims.

Although a good deal of preparatory work had been done—Coopers and Lybrand had already laid the options bare—the room for manoeuvre was severely limited. Sir Paul's majority, worn down by the effects of his party's policies and the government's unpopularity, had been reduced to the barest minimum, 31-30, a precarious position, made all the more so by the rebellious antics of some of his Tory group, facing a solid Labour opposition scenting victory: on this occasion a margin on which more than the future of a single school would rest; a far cry from the majorities of 45 and 57 when Peter Bowness was driving through his education changes. Sir Paul's tenuous hold on power—the next local elections were less than two years away—was not, therefore, the most propitious background against which to tackle the deeply rooted problems which waited amid the widespread sentiment within educational circles that the new authority would not succeed. 'Make sure you last two years,' was the at-the-time puzzling exhortation I had received from a fellow chief officer on my appointment. Its alarming import was to become all too clear in due course.

Apart from political uncertainty, other difficulties stood in the way of the changes Eddie Lister and Sir Paul wanted to see. The education service in Wandsworth had been the subject of a half-hearted reorganisation as recently as 1986, from which it had barely recovered. There is only so much schools and the general public can take; and there could no longer be the prospect of a wholesale 'top-down' programme of closures and reorganisation, of, for example, regrouping sixth-form work along tertiary college lines, an option ILEA had agonised over and rejected. Those days were gone. Any school not wanting to face change could seek to thwart its authority's intention simply by opting out to become grant-maintained. The new Wandsworth authority would have nothing like the powers of the authority it was replacing.

Eddie Lister and Sir Paul Beresford were more than equal to this challenge. Although, like Wandsworth itself, the two were routinely labelled as Thatcherite, on closer analysis this convenient but misleading oversimplification dissolved into something much more complicated, interesting and charged with the potential of even more radical change. Their brand of politics differed from conventional Thatcherism in two significant respects. First, they genuinely believed in local government, that the Town Hall could provide local services as well as any organisation, not necessarily in every case by direct labour using its own staff, but by the widest range of means as long as these did not involve rip-off merchants, self-serving monopolies or restrictive practices. In this, they departed markedly from Thatcherite orthodoxy in which there was no place for such an assertive version of local government. When one of the railway stations in Wandsworth was threatened with closure, they proposed that the council take it over. They were, in fact, reinventing municipal conservatism. Second, their approach to the provision of public services went further than the usual measures of competitive tendering, outsourcing and privatisation, which Wandsworth had pioneered and indeed had embedded in the government's psyche in the first place. The council's exceptional success in delivering better services at lower cost was due to a single-mindedness unique in local government in the degree to which it systematically applied the full force of business principles and practices to all aspects of its services and activities, an approach which came to be known as the 'Wandsworth Way'.

Eddie Lister and Sir Paul would not have had much time for a discussion about whether 'society' existed or not, nor for any such abstractions or dogma, whether from 'left' or 'right', that wished to see the state wither away. Whatever 'society' was, however, they were sure it could never be a reason to prevent people from making decisions they were perfectly able to make for themselves. They took great pains to identify the services the public wanted and needed and saw it as their job to provide these services at lowest cost. Will it work? was the test they constantly applied. They were not bottom-line bean counters. Quality, as much as price, was built into specifications, a discipline which was to have a profound effect on their latest responsibility, education. Financially, they had little to thank Mrs Thatcher for. The more efficient their council became, the less it received from the Treasury as the annual baselines on which its Rate Support Grant settlements were calculated successively fell. Once convinced, they were prepared to spend generously, as evidenced by their willingness to depart from the government's policies relating to the supply and demand of school places.

ILEA's Legacy: Opposition and All Change

Both Eddie Lister and Sir Paul Beresford were confident that their new style of local government could more than compensate for the fewer powers education authorities now had and that their distinctive free-market Toryism would provide the ideological and practical means by which ILEA's inheritance would be transformed. In their eyes, ILEA represented in concentrated form everything that was worst in the way public services should be provided—monopolistic, *dirigiste*, inflexible, expensive, and inefficient. In its time, ILEA had had every chance to provide a first-class service. It was a precepting authority; as such, it had access to greater financial resources than most. It was a single-purpose authority; education did not have to compete with other services to the same extent. In addition, unusually for such a public body, it was under the unchallenged control of one political party for the greater part of its life, enabling it to deploy resources more effectively and consistently over many years. As far as Eddie Lister and Sir Paul were concerned, its Labour leadership had abused its privileged position to impose on the capital an education system which fell far short of what was needed.

Their criticisms were legion. County Hall mistakenly thought it knew better than parents and pupils what kind of education they should have; the allocation of places was guided more by the needs of the school than the pupil; the natural and proper differences among children were not allowed to flourish; only one form of schooling was available; teaching was largely undifferentiated; extreme positions in theory and practice, barely indistinguishable from the left-wing dogma with which they were inseparably entwined, were unquestioningly preferred. Competition and the recognition and celebration of achievement, whether sporting or academic, were rarely to be found: everyone was to have prizes. A certain sameness had settled like a cloud on the comprehensive vision. Equality of opportunity had become hopelessly confused with uniformity of provision. ILEA seemed to be driven with something akin to messianic certainty by a tunnel vision of the world—intolerant, given to superior moralising, and insulated from outside challenge by its exceptional constitutional and financial arrangements and from self-doubt by inbred recruitment and advancement.

Such a view of ILEA was not recognised by the overwhelming majority of teachers in the borough. To many of them, ILEA was less an organisation than a belief system, which expected and received from them a degree of loyalty and commitment unusual in public service. ILEA was apart, above the machinery of local government into which they were now to be plunged—bad enough in itself, but Wandsworth! The council's misunderstanding or misrepresentation of ILEA's values, difficulties and achievements only went to show how unfitted its politicians were for their new responsibilities. Wandsworth's teachers were convinced they faced a return to a class-riven, devil-take-the-hindmost education system in which the well-off and the clever would benefit at the expense of the disadvantaged who would be left further behind. They had heartfelt answers to each of Wandsworth Council's criticisms. But they had lost the argument. The barbarians were at the gates. Of all the successor councils in inner London, Wandsworth's takeover was the one most feared by the teaching force. After decades of having everything their own way, Wandsworth's teachers were now to be managed by political rivals equally driven by ideology but an ideology opposed to everything they stood for in which empiricism, variety, competition, experiment, innovation, risk and distrust of theories and abstractions spurred their thoughts and actions, an ideology which could accept education as having an integrity and life of its own outside and beyond politics.

Although Eddie Lister's and Sir Paul's agenda was unexceptional enough—a greater role for parents, orderly schools, more traditional methods of teaching, concentration on basic skills, and the concepts of excellence and achievement restored—they departed from many of their own natural supporters as well as their opponents in the open-mindedness they brought to the possible measures whereby these aims could be met. They had no preconceived institutional answers, no hand-me-down, off-the-shelf nostrums. They were not impaled on selection nor hung up on sixth forms. Refreshingly, they realised there was no single magic bullet to get us out of the fix we were in. Education's problems were multifarious; solutions would need to be similarly varied.

There would be no meeting of minds between Wandsworth's teachers and their new political masters. Policy unfolded against a backdrop of reciprocating hostility. Although the physical violence which had resisted the sale of council houses in the 1980s never surfaced—the education reforms in prospect were seen by some as similar moves towards privatisation—raw emotions were never far away. Police were called to critical committee and council meetings and patrolled the corridors. If it was to be 'one of those evenings', we would not venture forth but stay in the building to avoid running the gauntlet of the crash barriers we could see being erected. As if this were not enough, there was the ever-present threat of time-consuming, enervating legal challenge. The words 'ten local government objectors' may be thought clear enough, but not so in the guerrilla nature of the times we were in. On their true meaning, eventually settled by a High Court ruling,[2] rested the legality of the contentious closure of a primary school, an example of the procedural eggshells we constantly had to tread. Nevertheless, the dripping of arguments into the stillness of the courtroom—'if your Lordship pleases'—was preferable to the sound and fury of the heaving picket lines outside the Town Hall.

Neither would there be any common ground between the Conservatives and their long-standing political opponents, who, in the early years of the new authority, were well supported, well organised and certain of the rightness of their cause. At the end of every public meeting, 'a member of the public' would rise to move a vote of no confidence in the council. Unfortunately, the Labour Party had nothing new to offer. At elections, it campaigned on the policy-free slogan 'Every School a Good School'. Its thinking seemed rooted to the spot, incapable of moving away from unquestioned orthodoxies. It did not seem to have shaken off the sentimental, defeatist, exculpatory attitudes of the 1960s: 'If a child comes late, it is not necessarily he who is to blame. If obscenities are used in the home we may expect obscene language from the child.'[3] Every educational issue seemed to be reduced to considerations of equity rather than effectiveness. Poor performance, while regrettable, could be forgiven or at least explained away if the teaching arrangements were judged to be fair. The sense and expression of outrage readily directed at any instance of perceived injustice never seemed to be aimed at ignorance itself. Criticism of teachers was not to be countenanced openly, an unhealthy state of affairs in nobody's interest.[4]

To its credit, the Labour Party did not argue for more resources, although understandably it was against anything which could be construed as 'cuts'. Neither did it have much time for the particularly vitriolic strain of trade unionism that characterised Wandsworth's teachers' associations at the time. In committee, its opposition was conducted with great courtesy, intellectual honesty and a depth of conviction one could only admire. The emptiness of its position, however, all too often took the form of a running, nitpicking procedural 'point of order, Mr Chairman' challenge, which kept the officials on their toes and in committee rooms after closing time but did little to advance the cause of education: 'The meeting ended at 10.29'. Whatever the Labour opposition had to say on any matter of substance was invariably little more than a reflex action to what the Conservatives put forward.

The knee-jerk reaction to an early decision to discontinue ILEA's policy of 'banding' gave a foretaste of the kind of reception which was to greet each and every change. Banding was an attempt to engineer, by allocating places according to pupils' abilities, an intake for each secondary school representing a cross section of the whole ability range—in ILEA's view, not shared by most authorities, the essential characteristic of a truly comprehensive school. For this purpose, assessment, roundly attacked for other organisational uses and in the hands of others, was considered permissible. Disregarding the new political unacceptability of such a policy, the decline in pupil numbers had severely weakened its effectiveness even in ILEA's terms, but that was not the point; to the Labour opposition, seemingly, the purity of principle was more important than practicality, however imperfect. Notwithstanding its protests, Wandsworth's parents would in future be invited to express three preferences for a school place, the intention being to meet as many of the first preferences as possible. In common with many of the new inner London authorities, Wandsworth wanted to give priority to the children of its own residents but was prevented in this by a High Court ruling, the *Greenwich Judgment*, which declared such a course of action illegal. The new authorities would have to accept, as before, children from across their boundaries, an additional element of competition not unwelcome to Wandsworth but, nevertheless, a complicating factor in planning.

The abandonment of banding had long been expected by the schools themselves and was viewed with equanimity. It caused waves only in Labour circles where with characteristic exaggeration it was seen quite mistakenly as the opening shot in a campaign to get rid of comprehensive education altogether. In the wider scheme of things, it was little more than a technical adjustment. Far bigger changes were on the horizon, of which the most important were not organisational, dealing with the effects of falling rolls on secondary schools, how many, how big and what kinds of schools there should be in the future, but cultural. With ILEA out of the way, the political, intellectual, philosophical and even pedagogic environment in which schools moved and had their being had abruptly changed. Within the new dispensation, schools would be expected to use their new self-governing powers to run themselves like other council services along sound management lines, not only in terms of finance, procurement and personnel, but in the quality of the education they offered. Schools' performances would be judged against objective criteria of pupil achievement and by the degree to which their admissions reflected parental approval.

A key component of the committee structure of the new authority, therefore, was the Performance and Standards Monitoring Group. Its remit, to evaluate 'standards of pupil performance; the quality of curricular and assessment arrangements; performance indicators; the organization and management of learning; governors' responses to inspection reports; the effectiveness of specific grant projects and in-service training', left no doubt where priorities lay. It would no longer be necessary for the public, politicians and the profession to depend on such judgments as 'the quality of school education in ILEA (is neither) wholly very good nor very bad. Primary education is reasonable, if not often exciting. The main weakness lies in secondary education, where there are causes for serious concern about standards in some schools and some subjects.'[5]

Headteachers adopted a more pragmatic approach than their staff. There was much in the new educational landscape that suited them. For one thing, they could now buy their own desks and they could always lead their schools out of Wandsworth's unwanted grip. The irony of the situation was not lost on observers; in its vendetta with local government, the government had offered a lifeline to the very kinds of school they most wished to see disappear. The heavily politicised governing bodies, on the other hand, were almost uniformly hostile to anything the council proposed. Some seemed to act like commissariats. On my first visit to one of the borough's most significant schools, the person rising from the headmaster's desk to greet me was the chairman of governors. He came in most days, I was told.

The governing bodies, particularly those of secondary schools suffering the effects of falling rolls, however, were on weak ground. People had been voting with their feet for years: 40 per cent of pupils leaving the borough's generally well-regarded primary schools preferred to go elsewhere, and 15 per cent of children of school age were educated in the private sector, twice the national average. Even ILEA's own inspectors had expressed concern at standards in the borough's secondary schools, whose overall performance was heavily dependent on that of a small minority. In 1989, 18 per cent of pupils left school without taking an examination in any subject, 35 per cent without taking mathematics, 23 per cent without taking English, and 15 per cent without taking any science subject. Only 26 per cent of sixteen-year-olds continued their education into the sixth form. Moreover, all these figures reflected worsening trends over a period of time; they were not provoked by the impending take-over. Nor was this record the result of a lack of resources. Other inner boroughs with higher indices of social need were turning in better figures. Wandsworth's unit costs were sky-high. ILEA's failure to deal decisively with the impact of falling rolls in the borough had meant that some 4000 places were unfilled at an unsustainable net cost of some £4 million per annum.

The stock-in-trade response to such a fall in demand, exacerbating the already deleterious effect of natural wastage, would have been a programme of closures and amalgamations. Although these would eventually play a part, albeit a small one, in Wandsworth's final scheme, Eddie Lister and Sir Paul Beresford resisted government pressure and the short-term temptation to sell off 'surplus' sites and buildings and thus kept their options open until their thinking became clearer. A succession of Conservative secretaries of state had failed to solve the policy contradiction between the need to make savings and the simultaneous wish to create greater choice by putting redundant places to more varied use. Eddie Lister and Sir Paul were to draw the proper conclusion from the vacant and emptying premises they had inherited in seeing them as opportunities to be developed, not assets to be stripped.

The Politicians Plan: Specialisation Makes Its Appearance: Magnet Schools

Wandsworth's underlying problem was not one of bookkeeping, of balancing supply and demand, but the failing effectiveness and subsequent unpopularity of the schools themselves. To reverse the trend and in the face of received wisdom that their newly acquired control of education portended a wholesale collapse of confidence in state education in the borough, Eddie Lister and Sir Paul Beresford decided to go for growth. First, they would boost recruitment at age eleven and the numbers staying on at age sixteen through increasing the attractiveness of Wandsworth's schools. Second, they would raise the levels of attainment through improving pupil motivation, identified as a key issue. Measurable performance targets were swiftly attached to enrolment, retention and test results, with the prospect of success rates in each being built into the formulae determining schools' financial arrangements with the council. But targets are not policy. It was quite another matter to formulate the means by which such aims would be achieved. Here, there was one previously unexamined strategy I thought might help—specialisation. It was this strand in our educational tradition that I invited the council to consider.

Traditionally, specialisation had occupied an inferior, even in the minds of some, a potentially damaging, place in the national education system. The overriding priority Sir Robert Morant had given to the values of a general, liberal, humane education had prevailed throughout all the major upheavals of the twentieth century, even the replacement of the tripartite by the utopian comprehensive system. His views that secondary schools should offer 'an approved Course of general instruction extending over at least four years' and that 'specialization . . . should only begin after the general education has been carried to a point at which . . . a certain solid basis for life has been laid' echoed down the generations and were carried forward into my own education and beyond.

In spite of this discouraging background, it was to specialisation that I now turned, with the example of the Royal Ballet School before me. Enabling schools to specialise while retaining the benefits of a broad liberal education within a comprehensive framework, could, I thought, provide an important means of reinstating a commitment to individual endeavour, success and excellence and of enabling children to go to schools more suitable to their talents beyond their immediate neighbourhoods if that were called for. The case for specialisation had been graphically put by the account given by David Hockney, the most illustrious of my schoolday contemporaries, of his experiences at *the* grammar school, to which he had won a scholarship:

> At Bradford Grammar School we had just an hour and a half of art classes a week in the first year; after that you went in for either classics or science or modern languages and you did not study art. I thought that was terrible. You could only study art if you were in the bottom form and did a general course. So I said Well, I'll be in the general form if you don't mind. It was quite easy to arrange, because if you did less work you were automatically put in that section. I remember

that the mathematics teacher used to have some little cacti on the windowsill; I always thought I never needed to listen in those classes, and I used to just sit at the back and secretly draw the cacti. Then they told me off for not doing much work, and the headmaster said Why are you so lazy? You got a scholarship. When I pointed out that I wanted to do art, they told me There's plenty of time for that *later*. Not the answer you give to somebody who's keen on any subject, I think. They probably wouldn't do it now.[6]

David's headmaster wrote to his father:

Dear Mr Hockney,

David's Form Master and those who teach him have been considering his future, and they think it worthwhile my writing to you to suggest that as his ability and keenness appear to be on the artistic side, he might suitably transfer, before long, to a School of Art, and there prepare himself for a career in some branch of drawing or painting.

I should like to know what you think of this suggestion and if you approve of it, at what age you think he should turn over to a more specialised form of education.

Yours sincerely,

R. B. Graham
Headmaster

Mr Hockney wrote to Bradford's director of education and received this answer:

Dear Sir,

Your application for permission to withdraw your son, David, from Bradford Grammar School in order that he might attend the Regional College of Art has been submitted to the Committee.

After careful consideration the Committee believed that your son's best interests would be served by completion of his course of general education before specializing in Art. They, therefore, were not prepared to grant your request.

> Your son should continue to attend the Bradford Grammar School
> in accordance with the terms of the undertaking you gave as a
> condition of his admission.
>
> Yours sincerely,
>
> A. Spalding
> Director of Education

I hope I avoided ever writing such a letter. Of course, not all children have David Hockney's talents, but every child can do something exceptionally well. Although this important truth had so far not been sufficiently reflected in our education system, it was being given pride of place in a new kind of school gaining popularity in the United States. Somewhat infelicitously named a 'magnet' school, it nevertheless, in its Yankee brashness, summed up Wandsworth's aim to improve its schools through putting their attractiveness to pupils and parents at the centre of its educational policy.

Magnet schools had their origin in the American Civil Rights movement of the 1960s and '70s as a major means of desegregation. By offering specialised programmes of study not available elsewhere while staying within the state system and continuing to cater to the needs of local children of all abilities, these new kinds of schools aimed to attract pupils from outside their immediate neighbourhoods. In so doing, the intention was to dilute the damaging and dangerous polarization taking place between black and white children, increasingly trapped in their often 'smokestack' catchment areas and to reduce the 'white, bright flight'. Magnet programmes took many forms. Some were simply intensifications of usual subjects, such as languages, information technology and the performing arts. Others were variations, often with a more vocational edge; TV production, tourism, and leisure and hospitality, for example. In certain places, they reflected the employment needs of their localities: in country and coastal areas, agricultural and marine studies; in Houston, unsurprisingly, meteorology and the space sciences. Magnet schools had the backing of the law. Court orders required schools to admit pupils of different racial origins and backgrounds who were bussed, free of charge, out of their districts and zones to others further afield. There was a second underlying agenda. Supporters argued that, by providing courses deliberately geared up to the talents and interests of pupils, *which they themselves could choose*, magnet schools would improve the incentive to learn and, thereby, lead to higher standards of attainment, better behaviour, less truancy and alienation, and a greater commitment to long-term learning. Released from the usual admission arrangements, magnet schools were encouraged to involve their communities and local businesses in their work, to innovate and experiment and to compete with each other, in particular to celebrate success and achievement.

By 1988, there were some 1500 magnet schools in the States. I had come to know about them first-hand through my involvement with the City Technology Colleges' Trust, set up under the chairmanship of Cyril Taylor to promote Kenneth Baker's CTC programme. Cyril put me in touch with leading activists in the States and arranged for me to take a small study party of Wandsworth's teachers and principals to America—immediately branded as a 'junket' by *The Wandsworth Guardian*—to see for ourselves. During February 1989, we visited magnet schools in three districts, all subject to desegregation orders. Two, Yonkers and East (Spanish) Harlem in New York, had falling rolls. One, in Miami, Dade County, had rising numbers. Of particular interest to us was the school we went to in Spanish Harlem's District 4, which had become a place of international pilgrimage in view of the dramatic improvements claimed there.

Wandsworth's teachers and principals reserved judgment on the merits of the magnet approach. One difficulty facing us all was coming to terms with the totally different cultural environment into which we had plunged. The problems facing our counterparts were familiar to those at home but on a scale outside the experience of any of us. In East Harlem, it was not unknown, we were told, for pupils as they sat at their desks to be relieved of items of clothing by poorer children. The superintendent of Dade County apologised for being late because there had been a classroom shooting incident in one of his schools. All the schools we visited were ringed with notices warning drug dealers of the higher penalties they faced if they were caught there; 25 per cent of New York's children were drug addicted at birth, and so on. London's problems of social deprivation appeared much diminished and more manageable in comparison. Understandably, our American friends seemed to have an altogether more urgent grasp of the dire nature of the challenges they faced and of the need to use the widest range of means to overcome them.

My travelling companions, no doubt the theology of the optimum size of all-ability schools going through their minds, stood aghast at the campus of thousands of pupils housed in different buildings under a multiplicity of different but complementary managements, schools within schools. What would Sir Keith have said? I made an envious mental note of the District whose schools, without any governing bodies, reported directly to their superintendent and his board of eight who managed a multi-million dollar budget. Our American hosts needed no convincing that their nation was at risk. Action was imperative and prosecuted with vitality and drive. They were willing to try new methods and to experiment, to take risks, to be as blunt about failure as success and seize any instrument near to hand to get results; to confront, challenge and exploit 'the system', and not as we were prone to do, just accept, interpret, adjust and navigate around it. Their can-do attitude—'we have no regulations only statistics'—highlighted in my mind the inadequacies of our response to our problems, deferential to the past, institutionally hidebound, hesitant, doctrinaire, imaginatively narrow, and if anything in spite of the liberalising 'market' rhetoric becoming more prescriptive. America's mind had not closed. Ours had.

A visit to a school in Miami made a lasting impression on me. I found myself in a classroom at the time when, every morning, children stand to salute the flag and recite the oath, hand on heart, something I was unprepared for and with which, like many of my similarly inhibited countrymen, I had a problem. I was not alone. A rather dishevelled youngster did not know what to do either. Unobtrusively, arm around him, his teacher whisperingly showed him what was expected. His new pupil, he told me afterwards, had just arrived on a boat as a refugee from Cuba. Through the windows, the sight of the giant Stars and Stripes flying from every building, which is such a feature of the United States, conveyed the self-confidence of a country for all its problems still on the move. I returned to England with a new determination to do as much as I could to loosen up the ironclad mindset we inhabited.

In my report, I wrote:

> The force of the magnet idea lies in the fact that it recognises
> more openly than our system has accepted so far that many

young people, particularly the less able and the more easily 'switched off', learn better and on a broader front when they are able to follow programmes in which they are naturally interested, which they have chosen for themselves, in which they can succeed and in which they can see a strong relationship to the world of work and to the prospect of employment.

Many magnet schools carried their commitment to the central importance of engaging the involvement of pupils in their own learning on their own terms into their teaching arrangements through an accelerated learning system known as 'tracking' whereby pupils progress through their studies at their own rate according to the graduated levels of attainment they achieve. HM Inspectorate in its contribution to the design of the national curriculum had introduced the idea of 'key stages' in a pupil's progression, each representing a level of competence which could be expected of the majority of children in each of the corresponding age ranges to which they belonged.[7] I thought this idea could be developed and put to beneficial use in timetabling as well as assessing pupils. Freeing children from the age-related as well as mixed-ability classes into which they were invariably put, regardless of their abilities and attainments, and allowing them to take greater control of their studies seemed to me something we should look at in our attack on low expectations and achievement. I put 'tracking' in my report.

The People Have Their Say

These ideas were well received by Eddie Lister, who was responsible for masterminding the new authority and its policies. He saw magnet courses and schools as valuable tools in introducing greater flexibility into the comprehensive ideal. Needless to say, they attracted the immediate and total hostility of the Labour Party. But why should they be over-concerned? The electoral tide nationally was flowing their way. Who knows, one of their considerations must have been, that within a month or two they would be back in control of Wandsworth Council—or sooner. I returned from my summer holidays to the bombshell news that a Conservative member of the council had died and with him the council's Conservative majority. There was to be a by-election in the Springfield ward at the end of the month. With the government's popularity plunging new depths there was every likelihood we would be facing a Labour administration within days.

Against all the odds, however, the Conservative candidate, Kathy Tracey, was returned with a majority larger than that of any other councillor, bigger even than the local MP's. She took her seat amid scenes of tribal jubilation and disbelief. Sir Paul Beresford almost tripped over himself to greet her with a giant bouquet. In the country, however, the electoral picture was not so rosy. The 2.2 per cent swing that had rescued the Tories in Wandsworth was nowhere else to be seen. During the spring of 1990, up to the elections for councils in London and the Metropolitan Districts due on 3 May, the government's prospects steadily worsened. 'The first three months of 1990 were an almost unmitigated disaster . . . just about anything that could go wrong did go wrong.'[8] The economy was again in recession. Unemployment, inflation, interest and mortgage rates, bankruptcies, and house repossessions all hit record highs. Reforms to the health service and education were generally not well received and seemed to be making little headway. Discontent found a flashpoint in opposition to the poll tax, which seemed to crystallise the failure of the government's approach to social and economic problems generally.

The brainchild of Kenneth Baker when he was minister for local government, the poll tax, like many reforms, looked all right on paper. It sought to introduce a fairer system of financing local government by replacing the rates, the property tax householders and businesses alone paid, with a charge levied on everyone who used the Town Hall's services. In practice, it proved a disaster. The new tax, coyly labelled 'community charge', never shook off its perceived basic unfairness in treating dukes and dustmen the same—although this was far from the case—and the amounts people were called upon to pay turned out to be far higher than they or indeed the government had expected. Widespread and bitter opposition ranged from non-payment campaigns to rioting in the streets, this time not in Doncaster or Rotherham but much nearer home, in Trafalgar Square. The blame was put squarely on 'the perversity, incompetence and often straightforward malice, of many local councils'.[9] How low the poll tax could be driven became the touchstone of politics. With some poetic justice, it fell to Kenneth Baker, now chairman of the Conservative Party, to salvage electorally what he could from the wreckage.

It seemed a hopeless task. Labour's lead doubled from 10.5 per cent in January to 21 per cent in March, a margin sufficient in that month to turn a Conservative majority of over 14000 in the Mid-Staffordshire constituency into a Labour majority of over 9000. By the time of the local elections, Labour's lead nationally had widened to 24 per cent and in London to a seemingly unassailable 28 per cent. In Wandsworth, the election was fought with unusual ferocity on one issue, the poll tax. The council had established for itself an unrivalled reputation for high quality services and low taxation. It had done all the government had asked of it and more. If a verdict were to be delivered on the government's underlying philosophy, it would be here. In canvassing literature, the divide between the two parties was dramatically illustrated by pictures of Hazelbourne Road, a street which separated Tory Wandsworth from Labour Lambeth, showing up the differences in what you got for Wandsworth's community charge of £148, the lowest in the country, and Lambeth's £496, among the highest. Nevertheless, in spite of this favourable scenario, as polling day approached, a 4 per cent swing against the Conservatives in the borough was confidently forecast. The Labour leader took me on one side in 'The Two Brewers' to tell me that, in the event of a Labour win, my services would no longer be required. Through the noisy, convivial fug, the significance of my friend's cheery warning to survive for two years shot into my mind as direct and sharp as the arrows being thrown at the dartboard nearby; I was about to lose my pension.

So it was with an unusual degree of attention that I took up my position in front of the TV set on election night to see the results come in, my mood darkening as a red stain seeped across London and Metropolitan England. Except, except: in the early hours; 'we have a report—unconfirmed—that the Conservatives have held Wandsworth with an increased majority'. Unconfirmed! Increased majority! But it was true. Foremost among a handful of councils, Wandsworth had defied the trend and returned Sir Paul's administration with a blistering majority of 35. In the morning, amid the debris of the count the night before, the Labour leader was nowhere to be seen.

The Conservative win gave a much needed boost to the new education authority and the stability and confidence to make the tough decisions that now needed to be made. The phoney war was over. Everyone now knew where he or she stood. There would be no return to ILEA's old ways as many had hoped. Those unsympathetic to the new regime would have to adjust. The council could now press on. By contrast, the government was in turmoil. Although the best gloss was put on the results, losses had been heavy. The days of the poll tax and of Margaret Thatcher as prime minister were numbered. During my remaining time at Wandsworth, there would be no fewer than three short-term education secretaries; John McGregor, Kenneth Clarke and John Patten, each grappling with the fallout of Kenneth Baker's Great Reform Act—the national curriculum, assessment and school autonomy.

The National Curriculum: 'The Sooner It Is Buried the Better'

> It always seemed to me that a small committee of good teachers ought to be able to pool their experience and write down a list of the topics and sources to be covered without too much difficulty. There ought to be plenty of scope left for the individual teacher to concentrate with children on the particular aspects of the subject in which he or she felt a special enthusiasm or interest. I had no wish to put good teachers in a straightjacket.[10]

Like many other people but with my Croydon experience behind me, I agreed with the prime minister. In the event, however, our somewhat naive expectations were cruelly betrayed. The national curriculum the government produced was, by general consent, a sprawling bureaucratic monster, over-elaborate, over-prescriptive and inimical to the best kind of teaching. This was not what I had campaigned and hoped for. In an article for *The Daily Mail* under the heading 'Stop This Juggernaught', I wrote: 'What we have now is not what was intended. Chickens are coming home to roost. The Government will have to rethink it on original lines. It is bureaucratic and unworkable. The sooner it is buried the better.'

My words were to prove a hostage to fortune and would themselves come home to roost later in the Court of Appeal.

In designing his national curriculum, Kenneth Baker was undoubtedly genuine in his belief that one of its main benefits would be to guarantee to all children a broad and balanced educational experience, a worthwhile ambition in itself. To his credit, he had successfully resisted Mrs Thatcher's efforts to limit it to no more than three 'core' subjects; English, mathematics and science. In this, he was surely right. Nonetheless, he principally saw the national curriculum as the means by which, for the first time in decades, a renewed sense of standards could be introduced throughout the education system. Since the comprehensive revolution, low or falling standards had been a familiar complaint, the grist of every educational debate. But where was the evidence? 'Who hath measured the ground?'[11]

Much of the criticism levelled at the education system was anecdotal, impressionistic and often little more than assertion. There was no framework of objective standards to which either the system's defenders or their opponents could appeal. It was useless looking to HM Inspectorate of Schools for reliable evidence. Such was the dominance of teachers' interests throughout the education system that inspectors' reports dealt solely with the adequacy of resources and gave opinions about the quality of teaching given. They had nothing whatsoever to say about the levels of learning achieved.[12] In the absence of such standards, pupils and their teachers were all too easily able to set their own; not surprisingly, these would often be too low. By laying down attainment targets describing the knowledge, skills and understanding pupils of different abilities and maturities can be expected to develop, Kenneth Baker intended to remedy this state of affairs. Such attainment targets would establish a repertoire of external expectations against which measurable performance could be set, neatly providing one of the most infuriatingly nebulous and out-of-control public services at long last with a mechanism of accountability and improvement. In principle, so far so good. The Croydon Curriculum had plumped for an entitlement of learning over the same ten subject areas about which there was little political or professional disagreement but had attempted to define attainment targets only in English, mathematics and science for assessment purposes.

Kenneth Baker dramatically and surprisingly broke completely new ground in two respects. First, he insisted that quantifiable attainment targets should be set across all the ten subject areas; second, that detailed 'programmes of study', in effect syllabuses necessary to achieve them, should also be laid down. Further complications arose from the 'strands' running through some of these syllabuses and the grouping of certain levels of attainment into 'profile components'. There was no need for this degree of elaboration or prescription. Good teachers simply do not teach like this. Kenneth Baker's own teachers at Hampton Grammar School and St Paul's would certainly not have accepted such a straightjacket. But then they taught in independent schools where standards were high and so would not have to! Teachers in the state system were in danger of becoming more akin to the paid-by-the-hour car assembly workers eschewed by Mr Justice Scott. The concept of attainment targets was sound; the extent of their proposed application was not. It was estimated that children in primary school would be confronted by over 1000 separate targets in one year. The amount of detail in the programmes of study was equally unnecessary. Much of the undoubtedly valuable work which went into their design could and should have been dealt with as a separate exercise and issued over time and in the light of experience as guidance and good practice. This would have been much more in the English tradition of leaving as much as possible to the discretion of the teacher and the school.

A more manageable and acceptable curriculum would have resulted had the planners—'ten ambitious quantity surveyors operating without the benefit of an architect'—restricted themselves to identifying 'the indispensable elements of knowledge',[13] the irreducible, unavoidable minimum required in each subject: *What Every Child Should Know.* Today, scientists are calling for more classroom attention to be paid to the certainties of gravity and oxidization than to environmental issues which change with the weather. During the formulation of our national curriculum, the more established counterparts of other continental countries were characteristically held up to unfavourable comparison because they were said to be inflexible and set in stone; they could not and did not keep pace with our rapidly changing times. This was simply because they, rightly in my opinion, concentrated on the essential and the unchanging. They were not sidetracked or swayed to the same extent by capricious *issues* or *themes*; multiculturalism, gender, personal health, economic understanding, environment, and citizenship, to name a few. The amount of organisational detail being embedded in our national curriculum would inevitably mean constant revision and review and unsettlement to the detriment of the service. The prime minister rightly recoiled in horror at a proposal that an additional 800 personnel should be appointed to maintain and police the national curriculum in addition to HM Inspectorate, who would in turn supervise them. Things had clearly got out of hand.

One of the reasons for the worst bureaucratic excess of the national curriculum was the degree of control exercised by the civil servants. Leaving aside the inevitably contradictory influence of their constitutional priority to look after their minister, temperamentally and by training they were wholly unsuitable to reform the work of teachers. On one occasion at a meeting at the DES, I asked for an explanation of the relationship between a certain programme of study and one of its levels of attainment. I was told they would be in the same ring-binder. Many of the attainment targets were the result of conciliatory draughtsmanship, rather than accurate reflections of political intention or good educational practice. In history, one of the original attainment targets, 'understanding history in its setting', gave way after a row to 'the knowledge and understanding of history'. A genuine effort to identify worthwhile educational aims and to introduce 'rigour' into the exercise became an exercise in semantics.

In designing the programmes of study, members of the subject working parties appointed for the purpose had inevitably split into the traditionalists (knowing facts) versus the progressives (finding out and practising skills). Naturally, measurable assessment lent itself more readily to the knowledge school of thought, particularly in maths, science and technology, where it was easily accepted. The extension of this overly quantifiable approach to all other subject areas was, however, pedagogically unsound; it was not in the best interest of the pupil, nor was it conducive to good teaching. As a result, much of the national curriculum was stricken by rigor mortis rather than infused by the rigour so commendably sought.

Where the strengths of the civil servants came into their own was their success in driving the bureaucratic process forward within the tight timetable set, a major factor in reconciling many of the academic differences involved, so that by the various appointed deadlines a national curriculum largely acceptable in terms of content had been agreed. As the various champions of their subject areas piled in to defend, and even seek to extend, their territory in the turf wars of the curricular working parties, problems of overcrowding were left to be sorted out later at leisure. Reducing the content of the national curriculum and streamlining its methods of assessment would be a major concern of John McGregor, Kenneth Clarke, John Patten, and their junior ministers. What would not command anything like the degree of support eventually forthcoming for the subject matter of the national curriculum were the methods of assessing the degree to which the attainment targets had been achieved which were simultaneously being developed. At the heart of the national curriculum, these were to develop into a major and serious battleground, imperilling the whole of the government's education revolution and throwing me, unwittingly, into the midst of the fray.

Testing, Testing

> As for testing, I always recognized that no snapshot of a child's, a class's or a school's performance, on a particular day was going to tell the whole truth. But tests did provide an independent outside check on what was happening. Nor did it seem to me that some children would know more than others was something to be shied away from. Of course, not every child had the same potential, and certainly not in every subject. But the purpose of testing was not to measure merit but knowledge and the capacity to apply it.[14]

Mrs Thatcher would not get the easily administered, simple 'snapshot' tests she wanted, which would tell at a glance how well a child was doing in relation to his or her abilities and in relation to everyone else in the same age range. In formulating an assessment system for the national curriculum, the planners again predictably fell into the two camps they had occupied in designing its content—the progressives and the traditionalists. As far as the progressives were concerned, the purpose of assessment was primarily diagnostic, or in the jargon, 'formative', designed to identify children's strengths and weaknesses and to show the way forward in their next stage of learning. Such subjective assessment was a matter between the pupil and the teacher and other professionals. The traditionalists, on the other hand, wanted pupils' performance to be assessed against objective criteria, on a pass-fail basis, by means of relatively simple pencil and paper, 'dipstick', 'litmus paper', standardised, in the jargon 'criterion-referenced', tests. Such tests would be similar, for example, to the grades people learning to play the piano are expected to pass regardless of their age. Only in this way, in the traditionalists' opinion, could a credible framework and sense of standards so far lacking in the state system be introduced.

Although purely diagnostic and criterion-reference tests would necessarily have to be different and kept apart, it was considered that a degree of common ground could be established between them using the idea already widely accepted within the key stages concept of a pupil's progression that certain levels of attainment could be defined by reference to what a pupil of average ability could reasonably be expected to know, do and understand within differing age ranges. It was this common ground that the working party charged with the task of designing an assessment system for the national curriculum, the Task Group on Assessment and Testing (affectionately known by its acronym TGAT) ambitiously sought to exploit. TGAT was under no illusion about the formidable intellectual and practical difficulties in its path. 'No system,' it acknowledged from the outset, 'has yet been constructed that meets all the criteria of progression (whereby test results relate to expected routes of educational development), moderation (whereby test results are enabled to be processed to allow comparison), formative and criterion-referenced assessment.' Unsurprisingly, it fell between all the stools and came up with a hugely complicated, labour-intensive and over-intellectualised scheme, which satisfied no one, its 'fake objectivity' roundly and authoritatively condemned. Bounced into accepting it, a 'thoroughly exasperated' Mrs Thatcher distanced herself from a system which was 'very different from what she had originally envisaged'.

Teachers were equally disenchanted. They had good reasons for questioning the intellectual soundness of the tests and the way results were to be reported. During the deliberations of the assessment working group, I had come to the view that keeping the four elements of assessment so far in play separate and not attempting a synthetic accommodation between all of them would be better. Rather, we should concentrate on the development of fewer and narrower standardised criterion-referenced, age-related tests, abandoning for this purpose the curriculum's over-elaborate sub-structure, and in particular, stripping out the confusing and complicating assumption that each level of attainment should be roughly equivalent to two-year's progression in a subject, a concept self-evidently as difficult to grasp as to administer. Brian Griffiths, the head of No. 10's Policy Unit, was receptive to these views, which would meet the prime minister's expectations, and I fed him ammunition in what became a barely concealed tug of war between Margaret Thatcher and Kenneth Baker. I found myself dictating the subtleties of age-related standardised tests to one of the 'Garden Girls' in No. 10's basement, and then explaining myself to an irritated Kenneth Baker, anxious to extinguish this source of resistance. The simpler route I proposed was not followed nationally. I would have to lower my sights and pursue my thinking closer to home.

Everyone subscribed to the ideal that testing should not determine what was taught; testing should arise from the course of studies followed. The chief objection to standardised age-related tests was that they would encourage 'teaching to the test' and so narrow learning to the detriment of the wider education sought. It was a criticism I did not accept. If society requires children to learn, do and understand certain things, it seemed unexceptional to me that they should be helped in this by being schooled to answer questions and undertake tasks showing whether they have done so or not. During my own education, what would be described as 'continuous assessment' was part of the warp and woof of the primary school day—so much so that no one attached much importance to it.

Tests were easily and frequently administered. At the end of each quiz, you would simply exchange your paper with the person sitting next to you, who would mark it according to the answers the teacher read out and then shout back your neighbour's results to be recorded. Hardly a day went by without a spelling bee (receive, receipt, niece; although, cough, plough) or mental arithmetic (for eleven-year-olds, the cost of three and a quarter pounds of bacon at one and tuppence a pound). At secondary school, parents were informed of progress by means of a termly report conveyed on one piece of paper, which in addition to brief comment, simply gave the percentage of marks gained in each subject and position in class. Also recorded was the number of times the child had been absent and late. At a glance, parents would know how their children were doing subject by subject and where they stood in relation to their peers. Whatever such reports lacked in the sophistication of today's anguished attempts at assessment, they were inexpensive, easy to administer and understand, and sufficient for their purpose.

To argue for standardised tests was to invite criticism that you were a Gradgrind—that you did not understand that education is not about filling buckets but lighting fires, that minds are not instruments to be sharpened but seedbeds to be cultivated, that you were the enemy of the imagination. It was never explained, however, why our period of greatest literary achievement occurred when teaching was at its most mechanical and didactic. William Shakespeare, whether a glover's son or, indeed Francis Bacon or the Earl of Essex, would have received the same classical education. Whatever little we know about his schooling, we can be sure he would not have followed a course in creative writing or Media Studies. Criticism of testing always seemed to be accompanied by an appeal to a superior view of education at its most indefinable. Education according to this thrust was concerned with the immeasurable; it was what remained after you had forgotten all you had been taught, that sort of thing, as if the utilitarian and the imponderable had nothing to do with each other, an approach sharply explored in Alan Bennett's entertaining play, *The History Boys*, to which I can readily relate, as it describes how working-class pupils of a northern grammar school are being prepared for Oxbridge.

The forces of darkness are represented by Irwin, who teaches to the tests awaiting students at university entrance by coaching his pupils in the tricks of passing exams and stands accused of betraying the higher purposes of education by the forces of enlightenment in the person of Hector. For Hector, 'All knowledge is precious whether or not it serves the slightest human need', as if the loss of Marie Antoinette's earrings is of the same consequence as the invention of penicillin or there is no difference between *The Book of Common Prayer* and the *Pigeon Fancier's*

Gazette. Getting pupils through their grades towards a school-leaving certificate and a job was to my mind every bit a part of education as turning them out to be well-balanced, fulfilled, decent individuals. I felt strongly that these two aims, so often captured by extreme theoreticians in the usual polarizing manner, were not mutually exclusive, nor were they necessarily inimical to each other, but could and should be reconciled by good teaching practice.

Years later, inspectors endorsed Wandsworth's insistence on objective—as far as it can be—testing and reporting, saying that it had been 'certainly right to have resisted the move by some head teachers to something akin to the traditional (subjective) and questionable "critical friend" approach to appraisal'. They concluded that Wandsworth's use of performance data was a key element in a well-conceived inspection and management strategy' and that 'the use of data to assess school performance against relevant comparators was better understood in Wandsworth than in most LEAs.'

A great deal of the credit for Wandsworth's acceptance of assessment, an enormous achievement considering ILEA's legacy, was due to John Burchill, who joined me from Croydon as chief inspector. His introduction and development of baseline testing, the capacity to track individual pupils from the beginning of their schooling through the key stages they would pass and, therefore, assess the 'value-added' at points of their education, came to have national significance. His ideas on reforming HM Inspectorate and restructuring the national system of school inspection were accepted by John Major's government.

Litigation—Again: This Time We Take the Teachers to Court

Where I thought the teachers' opposition to the assessment arrangements for the national curriculum fully justified was in the amount of almost entirely unproductive additional work it placed on them. For this reason, I was more than a little alarmed to be expected to provide the government with arguments in the Court of Appeal against one of the teachers' unions, the National Association of Schoolmasters/Union of Women Teachers, which was threatening to sabotage the tests in English, maths, science and technology scheduled to take place in June 1993 for fourteen-year-olds by boycotting parts of them on the ground of the excessive workload they entailed. The issue was obviously of critical importance to the government. If it could not apply its assessment arrangements, much of the purpose of the national curriculum fell away. And as assessment was, in law, an integral part of the curriculum, the possibility arose that the national curriculum itself, as drawn, may not be enforceable. The stakes could not have been higher. Who was deciding education policy—the government or the unions?

Prompted by ministers, Wandsworth had initiated action to try to prevent the union's partial boycott, arguing that, if it went ahead, its members would be in breach of contract and they and their union liable to a claim for damages. The union argued it had immunity from prosecution on the grounds that, as their dispute was a protest against the unreasonable amount of additional work they were being asked to undertake, it was a 'trade dispute', and as such, they were entitled to protection. The trial judge agreed. He ruled, 'The dispute was wholly or mainly about workload, or working hours. It is therefore wholly or mainly about terms and conditions of employment.' In effect the boycott was lawful. Again prompted by ministers, Wandsworth appealed the decision.[15]

In the Court of Appeal, the legal focus shifted from the role of the council to that of the government in the person of the secretary of state, who was responsible not only for teachers' terms and conditions of employment but the workload at the centre of the complaint. It would, however, be up to me to make the government's case. Evidence would be by affidavits, with the possibility of cross-examination, a disturbing prospect as I could not disagree with the union's calculations of workload, which they understandably dramatically portrayed. On one estimate, the amount of material associated with the national curriculum and assessment comprised twenty-six ring-binders containing 2560 pages, thirty proposals/consultation documents containing 3300 pages, Standard Assessment Tests folders totalling 500 pages and statutory guidance documents containing 1725 pages, giving a grand total of 8085 pages in all. 'The material continues to be produced.' And of course the union could not resist, again understandably, pointing out my concerns about the detailed and prescriptive nature of the national curriculum in my *Daily Mail* article. My chickens were coming home to roost with a vengeance.

So were Kenneth Baker's. At the same time as he was working on his national curriculum, he was giving teachers, as a palliative, much of what they wanted by introducing greater, and, it has to be said, much needed clarity into their working conditions. In future, teachers would be expected 'to be available for 1,265 hours in any year, together with such (unspecified) additional hours as may (reasonably) be needed to enable them to discharge their professional duties . . .'. No one had thought to ask, let alone answer, the question: Could the emerging national curriculum be taught within the teaching year?—an example of the much talked about 'joined-up government' if ever there was one. During its formulation, the national curriculum was commonly expected to take up to between 70 to 80 per cent of the time available. But this proportion had been settled on before the assessment arrangements had been developed and an estimate of their workload implications could be attempted. The NAS/UWT claimed that, in 1991, 'the average working week of secondary school teachers was 52 hours 44 minutes'. I could not disagree. I wanted to include in my evidence a categorical statement from the DES, on whose behalf I was effectively acting, that the requirements of the national curriculum and its assessment arrangements could be fulfilled and demonstrably so within the teachers' terms and conditions of employment. This was not forthcoming. I was in constant dread that, at any minute, I would be put on the stand to explain why Wandsworth had provided teachers with additional help to enable them to administer the disputed tests, effectively conceding the union's case. Why the NAS/ UWT did not use this clinching fact I have never been able to understand. I could not and did not contradict the union's workload argument and this was noted.

The best I could do was to argue that the union's complaint was not really about workload but about its longstanding antagonism to the concept of a national curriculum and its assessment—that their protest was not about the *amount* of work they were being required to undertake but about its subject matter, its *content*. To my mind, their game was given away by their protestations that they were not against the national curriculum and testing in principle, only those elements they considered 'unreasonable', 'unnecessary', 'inappropriate' and 'crude'. The arbiter of all these qualities would, of course, be the teachers themselves. We were heading back to the 1960s and Ronald Gould.

In his judgment, Lord Justice Neill said that I 'had put the matter succinctly', and referred to my central argument: 'The Union has never suggested that the terms and conditions of employment ought to be changed. Rather, it was complaining about the content of their jobs.' 'The arguments before us', his Lordship said, 'occupied several hours. In the end, the question to be determined is one of fact which has to be decided on the evidence contained in the Affidavits and in the documents.' On this basis, the judges had no option but to conclude that the dispute was a 'trade dispute'. The only comfort I could salvage from my efforts was the 'several hours' the judges had been caused to spend in considering whether, on a true construction of the matter, the union was, in reality, challenging government policy. I had done the best with a weak hand. At least it had not been a walkover. I could not disagree with the court's verdict and the reasons given.

Faced with the implications of the legality of the union's boycott, the government agreed to measures to reduce the teachers' workload, among them restricting testing to English, mathematics and science, *pace* the Croydon Curriculum and Margaret Thatcher. Although a period of relative calm ensued, the basic fault lines running through the assessment procedures remained unresolved. The SATs for fourteen-year-olds at the heart of the dispute were abolished a few years later.

'Diversity and Choice'

While the government's curricular and assessment plans were running into the sands, its drive to increase the number of CTCs and grant-maintained schools 'at a pace and in a way that would have spelt the end of LEAs in a matter of months', was equally making little headway. By 1990, less than half the fifteen CTCs planned had been established and fewer than thirty grant-maintained schools approved. Both kinds of school were procedurally difficult to set up. Sponsors were hard to find. With one or two courageous exceptions, the largest household-name companies could not risk involvement with such contentious politics. Most councils, some even Conservative, were hostile. Not so Wandsworth where the new authority could and was to be of greater help to the government. CTCs and grant-maintained schools were two important strands in Eddie Lister's policy towards secondary education in the borough, which was relaunched after his party's electoral win in 1990. Under this policy, he sought to replace, wholesale, the monopoly of neighbourhood schools Wandsworth had inherited with a range of genuinely different schools from which parents could choose the education they thought most suitable for their children. His slogan 'Diversity and Choice' was to provide the government with its own policy label—if not the policy itself.

Michael Ashcroft's[16] offer to sponsor a CTC in the empty premises of a vacated school was accepted and the college rapidly approved. At the crunch meeting at the DES, the mild-mannered John McGregor was no match for the businessman's negotiating skills: 'Do you want this f***ing million pounds or not, because I'm not going to look round another f***ing school!' The civil servants did not flinch. Another opportunity to establish a CTC presented itself at Battersea where the local comprehensive with fewer than 400 on roll was on the brink of closure, an eventuality that could not be allowed to happen, as the area was desperately in need of a good school. But we would need a sponsor.

Here Wandsworth's new brand of local government was to be put to the test. The council set about showing the same resourcefulness in saving Battersea Comprehensive as rescuing a railway station, but, fatally as it turned out, without the same freedom and powers as everyone else. With no time to spend searching for a sponsor, Wandsworth turned its attention to creating a new halfway house between the independent and public sectors by combining elements of the CTC and grant-maintained models and came up with the idea of establishing a selective technical college on a voluntary-aided basis. The council would act as promoter in the absence of any other, the role usually adopted for this kind of school by a Church of England or Roman Catholic body. Although such a school would be wholly maintained by the council, its governing body would be independent and in a better position to go down the grant-maintained route if it and parents so wished. The proposal engaged the country's most expensive legal minds. To no avail. A sympathetic

Kenneth Clarke, then education secretary, himself a QC, warned us privately and apologetically that Wandsworth's idea was held to be illegal. Intriguingly, the prospect of a selective school in one of the borough's most deprived areas had led to a surge of parental interest and expression of preference.

The government took fright. Clearly this was a step too far in the choice and diversity programme. Local councils were expected to retreat from the field, not advance. Legislation was to put the matter tersely beyond doubt. 'A local education authority may not establish a grant-maintained school.'[17] Shades of Shirley Williams and standardised tests! In one respect, however, the Battersea proposal had made its mark. The government's last piece of legislation deliberately opened up the possibility of wholly selective schools. The voluntary-aided model was conventionally used by the Southwark Diocese to establish a new Church of England school in empty buildings left behind by ILEA's last reorganisation to add to the existing denominational opportunities offered by two existing Roman Catholic schools.

Grant-maintained status proved to be the most ready-to-hand means of loosening up the system. Three schools, those with fewest problems, Graveney, Elliott, and an all-girls' school, Burntwood, voted to opt out. If they thought that, by doing so, they were frustrating the council's plans, they could not have been more mistaken. Their proposals were directly in line with Wandsworth's intentions. Up and down the country, education chairmen and directors were campaigning against grant-maintained status. The government deplored the extreme propaganda and tactics often used. In Wandsworth, by contrast, the chairman and director toured primary as well as secondary schools, promoting the idea, offering the council's continued no-hard-feelings support and help with negotiating the off-putting procedural maze involved. Government approval for Graveney's, Elliott's and Burntwood's proposals was promptly forthcoming. The prospects of the new schools were strengthened by the closure of two schools with hopelessly low numbers and poor enrolment, Walsingham and John Archer. Walsingham was an all-girls' school whose disappearance benefited Burntwood. Its closure was unsuccessfully contested in yet another High Court action on the grounds of reducing equal opportunities for all-girls' education.[18] The head of John Archer was a former colleague of mine at

Crown Woods. Going round his school with some awkwardness took me back to my own days as a teacher. Little seemed to have changed.

Alongside encouraging CTCs and grant-maintained schools, the magnet idea was firmed up. A practical objection to magnet schools and programmes was that there would not be enough time within the national curriculum for the degree of specialisation they entailed. Here, the first-hand expertise of Wandsworth's deputy, Hilary Nicholl, proved invaluable. Her previous position as headmistress of one of Kingston's most successful schools, Tiffin Girls' School, had done much to establish Wandsworth's credibility as a new education authority in the eyes of its teachers. She was later to go on to become the first head of the Schools Examinations and Assessment Council. Hilary was able to give convincing timetabled examples of how specialist courses could be fashioned within the framework of the national curriculum—avoiding the crude polarisation of my own education, a pitfall constantly in my mind. The design and accommodation of magnet programmes was made easier by ministers' decisions to lessen subject content and reduce the number of attainment targets, in particular, Kenneth Clarke's insistence on greater flexibility from age fourteen.

Cyril Taylor arranged for headteachers of magnet schools in New York to visit Wandsworth and talk about their experience. Two of the three remaining county schools with greater problems than their grant-maintained counterparts, Ernest Bevin, an all-boys' school, and Chestnut Grove accepted the council's proposals to become magnet schools. Ernest Bevin would offer specialist courses in mathematics, science and technology, with an emphasis on engineering and business administration. Chestnut Grove would offer art and design and modern languages. Each school would annually 'reserve a number of places, a quota, which may in aggregate be the majority of places for prospective pupils wishing to follow each specialised course, such pupils to be admitted by reference to their suitability to benefit from the course, their aptitude, which would be tested'.

Predictably, it was this characteristic of selection that aroused the opposition of the Labour Party in Wandsworth, although leading members of ILEA in its final months had begun to question the need to maintain so strictly the hegemony of their particular brand of 'banded' comprehensive school. Neil Fletcher, briefly ILEA's chairman, was quite open about the need to think afresh. He asked:

> What are the solutions [to the palpable failure of the comprehensive dream]? . . . One might be magnet or specialist schools. I fail to see the idea is anathema to many of my colleagues in the Labour Party. Why should not every school go ahead and develop a particular specialism in computers, sport, science, or languages, for example? Give pupils and parents a chance to choose the schools they prefer.

Mr Fletcher's flirtation with the magnet idea, however, came to nothing. The old guard at County Hall would have none of it; neither would the Labour Party in Wandsworth, which was vigorous in its opposition.

It was not, in my view, only selection which fuelled the Labour Party's antagonism. There were to my mind deeper reasons. Magnet schools and programmes appealed to those talents and abilities which marked pupils out from each other; the current brand of socialism could not cope with difference: *'Chacun doit être a portée de recevoir l'education qui lui est propre'.*[19] If this founding principle of the post-war system were ever to be fulfilled, the particular interests, gifts and strengths of children should surely be given every opportunity to flourish.

Nothing, however, it seemed could shake the Labour Party's conviction that selection, even self-selection, the core principle of the magnet idea, was inseparable from the elitism, unfairness and social divisiveness that had disfigured the post-war tripartite system. I did not agree. Magnet schools would not concentrate on the bright minority at the expense of the less able majority. Quite the reverse. Through the spread of specialisms on offer, they were aimed at capturing the attention and talents of every pupil. Magnet schools would remain comprehensive and serve their local communities. Testing would be used purely to enable candidates for specialist courses to benefit from them. It was hard to see why ILEA's system of testing in order to enable County Hall to allocate places according to the needs of the school and the ideological laboratory it represented should be seen as occupying the high moral ground in this respect. Why should allocation by officialdom be superior to attraction, providing parents and pupils with choices? We were never told. 'Children are not iron filings' was the witty accusation. Attacks on the associated idea of 'tracking' gave a particularly illuminating insight into Labour's thinking, which saw it as a means of keeping less able children 'down'. It seemed to me that the widely accepted differences in understanding and skills which can exist among children of the same age—as much as the often quoted seven years' in the case of mathematics, for example—was evidence enough, if evidence were needed, of the advantages of teaching children at their stage of development. Tracking merely recognised the natural and proper differences among children and enabled each to be educated at his or her own level, a proposition I thought pretty unassailable from any political perspective, even if this meant some pupils racing 'ahead' of others in terms of age.

It was true that specialised courses would, by their very nature, need enhanced facilities in accommodation, equipment, and personnel; Wandsworth had set aside £10 million for this purpose. As long, however, as these were available to all children on merit and on an equal footing, it is hard to substantiate the charge of unfairness routinely linked to the accusation that magnet schools would promote inequality and be 'divisive', the old catch-all criticism levelled at any departure however slight from the single ILEA model of comprehensiveness. The fact of the matter was that very great differences and inequalities between schools existed in ILEA's comprehensive system, which, in spite of commendable effort and considerable organisational advantages, the authority had proved unsuccessful in eradicating. ILEA's failure in this respect was to provide the marketeers with a persuasive example of the ineffectiveness of top-down systems, however powerful, to eliminate the inequalities they themselves were accused of fostering.

No one responsible for education policy in Wandsworth imagined that magnet schools or programmes or any such other structural changes alone would provide the long-sought answers to the education service's deeply rooted problems and seemingly irremediably poor performance. It would be many years before Battersea, for example, would overcome its difficulties. But there was conviction that progress, in whatever shape or form, would not come until we had escaped the stultifying effect of a system resistant to new ideas and change. Magnet schools and programmes, alongside CCTs and grant-maintained schools, would, if nothing else, help to challenge received orthodoxies, break up the old statism and contribute to a new culture of open-mindedness and fresh thinking.

Within four years, of the eleven maintained schools Wandsworth inherited from ILEA, only one, Southfields, decided to retain its neighbourhood comprehensive character and remained recognisable in its original form. Two new schools, one a CTC, the other denominational, had replaced two which had closed. Five had become grant-maintained. Two were offering magnet programmes to a selective entry. One had become a specialist technical school. A school sharing its premises with the *Lycée Charles de Gaulle* offered an *entrée* to a completely different educational tradition and experience. In large measure, Eddie Lister's vision was being realised. But rapid results could not be expected; so many variable and long-term factors were in play. Like everyone else in education, we were more in the business of sowing rather than reaping. Neither of us could nor sought to take credit for the signs of progress that were beginning to show through before I left. Wandsworth's results were improving at a greater rate than those of the rest of the country; in terms of GCSE results, the borough had moved from eighth to third position in inner London. I have no doubt, however, that, had the statistics been moving in the opposite direction, responsibility for them would have been laid squarely at our door. By the year 2000, it was possible to gauge some idea of the difference Eddie Lister's policies were having. He and my successor, Paul Robinson, would have cause to be pleased with the unusually full-blooded endorsement they received from the Office for Standards in Education in their first inspection of the authority that year.

> Wandsworth moved towards a more modern relationship with its schools well before most LEAs, a move that was not universally popular . . . The LEA has benefited from stable political leadership which has been (and remains) both clear as to principle and appropriately pragmatic in application. The 'Wandsworth way' represents a distinctive style and ethos, and in detail includes several of the strategies piloted

> in Wandsworth which are now embedded in the national standards agenda. Challenging schools to raise standards whilst promoting their autonomy in an education service that encourages diversity and increases parental choice are key objectives for education in Wandsworth . . . Attainment both on entry to schools and later is generally high for London . . .

> This report makes a number of recommendations directed for the most part to the improvement of what is already satisfactory or good. The LEA is in good shape to implement these recommendations and needs to make no major changes. The parents, pupils and schools in Wandsworth are well served.

Nobody could argue that the abolition of ILEA had been the disaster so confidently predicted.

Specialisation Takes Centre Stage

By the early 1990s, maximising children's differing strengths by providing them with the corresponding opportunities to express and develop them seemed not only unexceptional but necessary if children were to realise their full potential, the goal to which everyone had subscribed for generations but which had eluded even the comprehensive dream. It was a view shared by the new prime minister, John Major. His replacement of Margaret Thatcher shortly after the local election debacle of May 1990 did nothing to lessen the Thatcherite revolution in education, nor did it interrupt my association with No. 10, which continued when Nick True[20] took over the Prime Minister's Policy Unit from Brian Griffiths, who went off to sort out the national assessment and examination system, taking Hilary Nicholl with him. I was sent the draft of the first speech on education Mr Major was to give as prime minister for my comments. My initial alarm that No. 10's Old Etonian speech writer had appropriated William Forster's Education Act to one of Disraeli's administrations in the first paragraph increased as I read on through numerous solecisms—unvarying references to 'headmasters'—and passages ripe for improvement. Reworked drafts shuttled to and fro, my magnificent PA, Marilyn Daniels, feeding the fax machine like a stoker, until later in the evening it packed up, like all of us, exhausted. The final version, couriered to No. 10 in dramatic fashion by motor bike through sleeping streets, was delivered with characteristic understatement by the prime minister at the Café Royal the next day. I was pleased to hear his endorsement of Wandsworth's unfolding programme of different schools.

John Patten, John Major's education secretary, was keenly aware of the contribution specialisation could make to the diversity and choice agenda. In an article for the *New Statesman and Society*, he wrote:

> Selection is not and should not be a great issue of the 1990s as it was in the 1960s. The S-word for all socialists to come to terms with is rather specialisation. The fact is that children excel at different things; it is foolish to ignore it, and some schools may wish specifically to cater for these differences. Such schools are already emerging. They will, as much more than mere exotic boutiques, increasingly populate the educational landscape of Britain at the end of the century, a century that introduced universal education at the outset; then tried to grade children like vegetables; then tried to treat them . . . like identical vegetables; and which never ever gave them the equality of intellectual nourishment that is now being offered by the national curriculum, encouraged by testing, audited by regular inspection.[21]

Specialisation was to be one of the 'imperatives of the 1990s',[22] set out in John Patten's White Paper *Choice and Diversity*, published in July 1992: 'High standards will be fostered through testing, specialization, rigorous inspection and an ever-deepening recognition of the needs of individual pupils.' 'Children themselves as they get older and mature often have a well-developed sense of their needs.' The means whereby specialisation was to be encouraged and the wider choice and diversity programme advanced were to be set out in legislation the following year. Beneath its purely educational provisions, however, the 1993 Education Act, like the 1988 Act before, had a deeper purpose. It was to sound the death knell of education's time-honoured place in local government.

Donald Naismith

The End of the Local Education Authority

The stated aim of the 1993 Education Act, the longest Education Act ever to reach the statute book, was to 'improve standards, encourage diversity and increase opportunities for choice'. It was also intended 'to mark . . . the end of the long-standing local education monopoly of state school provision'. Procedures for opting out were streamlined. School autonomy was strengthened. Local authorities' functions were transferred to quangos; responsibility for sixth-form and Further Education colleges had been removed the year before. As an increasing number of schools opted out—the wholly unrealistic aim was that, by 1996, most maintained secondary schools would be grant-maintained—new arrangements would need to be made for their financing and supervision. For this purpose, a new body, the Funding Authority for Schools, under the direction of the government, would be established to share the local authorities' basic and previously unchallenged responsibility for providing sufficient school places in their areas. After certain thresholds had been reached, the FAS would take over altogether.

Alive to the danger that a stampede towards greater school independence would lead to even greater inequalities among schools now reflecting the acknowledged growth of wider social inequalities resulting from Margaret Thatcher's policies, the government took greater powers to protect against underperforming schools by reinforcing inspection and redoubling its campaign to eliminate redundant places. The inspectorate had been reformed the previous year along lines suggested by John Burchill, enabling a new regulatory body, OFSTED, to employ private contractors to inspect schools—a measure I had not supported. It was now given additional powers through 'special measures' to tackle schools 'at risk'. In certain circumstances, such schools could be taken out of LEA control altogether and put under new bodies, Education Associations, charged with the task of turning them round; that is, of course, if the schools were not closed down. The government's exasperation at the local authorities' perceived failure to deal with both issues, failing schools and surplus places, was expressed in the secretary of state's new breathtaking power to make and implement, subject to public enquiry, his own proposals to 'rationalise' a local authority's provision.

Local authorities were now to be replaced as partners in the secretary of state's duty to promote the nation's education by 'bodies in receipt of public funds'. In Mr Patten's view, local authorities should increasingly concentrate on 'those functions for which an LEA is best fitted; for example assessing and statementing pupils with special education needs and enforcing school attendance'. For me, the last straw was the removal of the statutory duty of councils to establish education committees.

Who was I to complain? I had long supported the view that schools should be able to exercise the greatest possible degree of autonomy within a loose framework of curricular regulation and that parents who were unable to buy the preferred education for their children should be placed as far as possible in the position of those who could. But I knew all too well that neither 'parental choice' nor 'the market' would have given me the education I had been fortunate to receive, which had been down to the tedious grind of local administration so often belittled and laughed at, regulations, officials, agenda, reports, committees, even the 'Points of order, Mr Chairman'. Drudgery divine, of a kind. In spite of the huge improvements in social conditions since that time, many youngsters would still and always be in the same position as myself as a child, dependent on, for want of a better word, 'the Town Hall' now defunct; the education service of my adopted city of Bradford of all places, which had given the country universal education, sold off, lock, stock and barrel, to an 'outsourcing company'. My old office in the Town Hall, where I had started out on my administrative career, now looked onto a Victorian landscape laid waste by 'developers' and an educational landscape equally devastated, in which there was no longer the need for an education officer. It was time to *cultiver mon jardin*, and to find out, at last, what had in fact happened after the Industrial Revolution.

POSTSCRIPT

Unfinished Business

*There must be a beginning of any great matter but the
continuing unto the end until it be thoroughly finished yieldeth
the true glory.*

Sir Francis Drake

All the key elements of Margaret Thatcher's education revolution were
adopted by every successive government of both parties and carried
forward into their policies to become embedded in the new orthodoxy
of the time. What was out of the question for Mr Callaghan's education
secretary had become 'not negotiable' for Mr Blair's.[1]

There was no counter-revolution. More powers and responsibilities were
given to schools, their self-government and independence reinforced.
Specialisation was more actively pursued than ever. The siege was
lifted from grammar schools, which became a protected species. More
new kinds of schools appeared on the scene; academies, free schools,
foundation schools, barely different from the CTCs and grant-maintained
schools they replaced. New ways of setting up schools involving parents
for the first time were introduced. Parents' rights were strengthened in
the pursuit of greater choice and accountability. Business and industry
took on a more prominent role, and barely disguised techniques of
privatisation employed. The national curriculum now stipulated not

only which subjects should be taught but, in the case of languages and mathematics, how they should be taught. The internal organisation of schools was not immune; setting was recommended. Targets were added to assessment, which now aimed to show the rate of progress as well as absolute levels of achievement. LEAs were sidestepped wherever possible, their powers reduced to regulation and commissioning, their duties on occasion even put out to tender and contract. As if to leave nobody in any doubt about the government's attitude and intentions towards them, the word 'education' was removed from the designation 'local authority'.

In spite of all these measures, the state system remains in all its essentials the 'compulsory, coerced, conscripted' system excoriated by Sir Keith Joseph, less so perhaps but still nonetheless firmly within the command and control mindset. Regardless of the liberating rhetoric, nothing of any significance can be done without Whitehall's say-so. 'Free schools' are 'approved'. Regulation piled upon regulation conditions every activity. Breaking the mould is slow, contentious, expensive and time-consuming. Notwithstanding a constant stream of 'reforms' along market lines and increased expenditure on a barely imaginable scale, costs have risen while standards have not. We languish in international tables. More parents fail to get their children places at the schools of their choice than ever before. School admissions have all too often become a squalid manoeuvre, at times attracting the heavy-handed attention of the law. Truancy rates and exclusions show no improvement and remain shamefully and unacceptably high. Social mobility has shuddered to a halt. The number of unemployable youngsters leaving school continues to defy belief.

Evidence, if evidence were needed, say the critics, that Mrs Thatcher's market strategy had got it spectacularly wrong. Proof certain, counter her protagonists, that her revolutionary instincts and ideas have not yet been carried through to their logical conclusion and that real progress will come only if central government swallows the same medicine it prescribed for local government and steps aside to create a genuine demand-led market in which more providers offering even greater diversity and choice are actively facilitated, parents and pupils are given a truly realistic say in their education, and schools are provided with tools adequate to the task of responding to their needs and wishes. During the years of our country's most rapid commercial and industrial growth and expansion, England had no national education system. A surprising number of our greatest explorers, inventors and entrepreneurs were either self-taught or were educated outside the formal structures of the day—Sir Francis Drake probably among them. They serve as powerful reminders of the depth of latent native talent waiting to be released from the dependence we have developed on organisations provided exclusively by the state.[2]

Improvement will come not through constant direction and hectoring from above but from the encouragement of incentive at every level, the achievement of goals replacing the deeply rooted obsession with length of study, as the basis of educational planning. One of the earliest purposes of the national compulsory system was to improve the safety and welfare of young people by taking them off the streets and disciplining them through collective experience; in more recent times through repeatedly raising the school-leaving age and creating new categories of study and training—regardless of expense and results—to manage the employment figures. Replacing attendance with performance requirements would lead to higher standards and reduced costs, both conflicting imperatives for the future, at present defying solution.

If schools are to be realistically held to account for their results, their outcomes, they must surely be given unfettered control of their inputs, including intake. Part, at least, of the higher expenditure which will always be sought should be found by allowing schools to supplement their per capita government precepts through charging fees and being able to make a profit. There would also seem to be no reason why 'payment by results' (little more than the flip-side of buying a private education) now firmly entrenched in policies aimed at reducing unemployment and repeat offending should not be revisited as a possible response where everything else has failed. Exaggerated scruples about vouchers should be overcome, and the example of their successful use in the United States followed,[3] not as an all-or-nothing policy option but as a valuable supplementary measure to raise additional money and improve choice. Further resources and operational flexibility would come through school-based contracts and wage levels in place of hidebound national conditions and pay scales which inhibit working practices and depress salaries.

In this scenario, the state would retreat in all organisational and curricular matters to the furthest margins consistent with securing its core interests; the need to safeguard those who would not fare well in such a competitive environment among them, entrusted to a reinvented, reconstructed and reinvigorated local government, able to exercise the same energy, commitment and resourcefulness shown by such authorities as Bradford at the beginning of the twentieth century and Wandsworth at the end.

The unhappy, ramshackle collection of half-baked constitutional experiments and confusing agencies, the results of central government's unremitting vendetta, which passes for local government today, neither particularly efficient nor democratic, cries out for reform on its own account. With education, it shares the same fatal lack of unifying principle, common purpose and coherent organisation. It is hard to imagine that such a state of affairs can last indefinitely. Although the completion of the free-market agenda in both is by no means inevitable, it would now be near impossible to recover the ground already yielded to the marketeers. The temper of the times, generally in all matters affecting the public services, is against top-down, take-it-or-leave-it *dirigisme*, and in education there is no appetite to return to the lowest common denominator as a guiding principle of policy.

In Victorian times, local government, through its school boards and local councils, was called upon to 'fill up the gaps'[4] on behalf of those children who were left behind by the main providers of the time, religious institutions. In this, they could have achieved so much more with government backing not hindrance. If reconstituted to 'fill up the gaps' left by the education market to ensure that its benefits are equally shared by all, local councils this time round would need the same competitive powers and competencies as everyone else. In viewing local government as irredeemably and inherently obstructive, Mrs Thatcher was mistaken. Her revolution would have made more headway had it enlisted the same capacity for innovation and cooperation shown by such local councils as Richmond, Croydon and Wandsworth and many others. As it is, local government and education still remain high on the list of matters about which 'something must be done'.

THE GILLIAN WARD CASE

The Gillian Ward case, which hit the headlines in 1971, was the appeal of a student against her expulsion, for which I hold myself largely responsible, from Bradford's Margaret Macmillan Teacher Training College, an unexpected outcome I regretted then and have done ever since; at the time, new to the job of assistant education officer for further education, I did not think anyone would pay much attention to what I had to say. *Ward v Bradford Corporation* was the first of seven occasions I was to find myself in the High Court in one shape or form, and although uncomfortable at the time it alerted me to the need to be scrupulously exact in all administrative affairs: 'How will this look in court?' I would often ask myself.

Gillian Ward was one of four students found with men staying in their rooms against the rules. The principal, Miss Goodison, had reprimanded and fined them. There the matter would have rested had not the news reached the local newspaper, the splendid *Telegraph and Argus*, and had been seized on by an up and coming left-wing journalist, Paul Foot. Councillors took a dim view of the whole episode, not so much on grounds of impropriety but because they had been kept in the dark and made to look fools. Wider issues, however, than the councillors' *amour propre* were at stake. The government was in the process of giving all Further Education colleges greater independence from their maintaining authorities. Margaret Macmillan had recently been granted a new Instrument and Articles of Government conferring wider powers over its day to day affairs. Councillors no longer had a majority on its governing body. Miss Goodison was one of a new breed of strong-minded heads, all too ready to take advantage of their newly-found freedom from local government regulations and to flex their muscles. Who was running the college: the council or Miss Goodison?

There was another issue. Ill-discipline in schools and colleges was becoming a major concern. The Gillian Ward affair took place against a background of widespread student unrest and militancy, spilling over from the 60s. Then, throughout Europe, students had been on the march, most dramatically in Paris where they had almost brought down the government. Students in Bradford posed a reassuringly lesser threat. A number from the Regional College of Art (as part of their Complementary Studies!) had taken to the streets to re-enact the Bolshevik Revolution, 'attacking' buildings 'taken over' by the 'provisional government'. Recently at Margaret Macmillan, Michael Duane, the former head of Risinghill, one of London's showcase comprehensives, closed down because of the anarchy for which it had become a by-word, had addressed the Students' Union. I was dispatched to a meeting of the governing body at Macmillan to find out what was going on and to do something about it.

There I found matters in disarray. The governing body, specifically responsible for discipline at the college, had equally been taken by surprise. All they knew was what they had read in the newspapers. They wanted to know more. How long had this been going on? How widespread was the problem? They thought that the case of the four students should be considered by their disciplinary committee provided for in the Articles of Government. To their discomfiture, they discovered that their disciplinary committee did not exist; they had failed to set one up. In addition, under the rules now coming into ever sharper focus as the small print was more closely examined, only the principal could refer cases to the disciplinary body, and this she refused to do!

Whatever arrangements the governors were minded to make to deal with future cases, surely the matter in hand would need to be left where it was. How could the students receive a fair hearing from governors who had already discussed their cases, and had not the students been properly punished? Such niceties, however, did not weigh with the councillors nor the governors now alarmed at their weakness in a tug of war with an obdurate principal. The governors set up a disciplinary committee, changed the rules to enable themselves as well as the principal to refer cases to it, and, acting on this new authority, dealt with the alleged offences of the four students accordingly.

The disciplinary committee, which I attended, duly heard the cases. It was clear that Gillian Ward's offence stood out from those of the others and as such, I pointed out, deserved a greater penalty. The governors decided on expulsion. Gillian Ward sought an injunction on the grounds, *inter alia*, of procedural irregularities, not least my participation. In this she failed, but appealed the decision. Her case was heard and dismissed by the Court of Appeal presided over by Lord Denning, Master of the Rolls. I was not in court to hear the judgment. The corporation was represented by the sure-footed assistant town clerk, John Stanbury, who had skilfully guided the council throughout and who now relayed their Lordships' findings by telephone as they unfolded, among them that although I had almost over-stepped the mark, I had done nothing to invalidate the proceedings. I was off the hook. Lord Denning's judgment was widely criticised for its tolerance of admitted procedural failings and for the personal strictures he levelled at the unfortunate Gillian Ward: 'She would never make a teacher. No parent would knowingly entrust their child to her care.' Whatever the reaction of the legal profession and the predictable outrage of student opinion, as far as the council was concerned a welcome measure of assertiveness had at last been introduced into the inchoate world of Further Education.

'The Croydon Curriculum: The Curriculum: Towards A Common Approach: Statement of Policy adopted by Croydon Council July 1984

This paper sets out the Croydon Education Authority's policy towards what is taught in the schools for which it is completely responsible. Its aim is to guarantee to all pupils, whichever schools they go to, the best possible all round education which will enable them when they leave to fulfil themselves as individuals, to earn their living and to play their part in a democratic society.

This statement does not describe the curriculum to be followed by individual pupils nor does it constitute the syllabus of teaching subjects. These are both properly matters for each school to decide in the light of the needs of their pupils as are the methods and materials of teaching to be employed and the way the school is organised and managed. It does, however, establish the overall aims all schools are expected to meet in their own way on behalf of each of their pupils. I hope it will enable everyone concerned with education to play his part in a better informed way and that, in particular, parents will be helped in supporting their children through having a clear idea of the aims of schools.

The dangers and limitations of such a statement are, however, well known. It is difficult to write about education in terms which can be widely understood and which the professional finds accurate. Establishing minimum requirements carries the risk of lowering expectations and discouraging worthwhile innovation and experimentation. If care is not taken standards can be the victim of standardisation. Many of the most valuable and lasting qualities of school life are not easily written down and do not in any case belong to the formal curriculum. The shorthand use of the names of traditional subjects can, if misunderstood, reinforce irrelevant and out of date demarcations. Above all the vital idea that learning is experience might be weakened.

The Committee is confident that, in practice, the teachers, on whom the quality of education finally depends, will not allow these fears to be fulfilled, and will use the statement as the source of help and support it is intended to be. For its part the Committee recognises that there is more to going to school than can be written down in statements of this kind. It is firmly committed to the pursuit of excellence and to individuality of approach both on the part of the school and the teacher. It is also committed to the continual development of the curriculum and to the introduction of new and better methods of learning and teaching wherever possible, and has made arrangements for these guidelines to be kept up to date.

Above all it looks to each school in planning its curriculum to interpret the aims set out in this statement in ways which will ensure that every pupil is introduced to the main areas of human experience and offered progressive advancement in each.

D R Loughborough
Chairman,
Education Committee

THE AIMS OF SCHOOLS

The overriding aims of all schools for their pupils are

1. to acquire knowledge, skills and practical abilities and the will to use them;

2. to develop qualities of mind, body, spirit, feeling and imagination;

3. to appreciate human achievements in Art, Music, Science, Technology and Literature;

4. to acquire an understanding of the social, economic and political order and a reasoned set of attitudes, values and beliefs;

5. to prepare for their adult lives at home, at work and leisure and at large as consumers and citizens;

6. to develop a sense of self respect, a capacity to live as independent, self-motivated adults and the ability to work together.

THE CURRICULUM

The curriculum is the means whereby these aims are achieved.

The Nature of the Curriculum

It is important that the curriculum is seen as the whole learning experience offered by a school. It includes those activities which take place outside the normal school day as well as those which appear on the timetable. It includes learning by precept and example as well as by formal instruction, and it is as much concerned with the ethos and approach of the school as a living community as with the lessons of individual teachers. Above all it is the means by which all pupils at every stage of their education are introduced to the major areas of human experience in a balanced, coherent and challenging way.

H.M. Inspectorate have provided the following description of the areas of experience to be reflected in the curriculum of schools.

1. Aesthetic and Creative

   The aesthetic area is concerned with an awareness of degrees of quality and an appreciation of beauty; the ability to perceive and respond both emotionally and intellectually to sensory experience; the knowledge and skills that may inform and enhance such experience and their expression; the exploration and understanding of feeling and the conscious recognition of intuitive response and action. The creative aspect is concerned with invention and may be the more active part of the aesthetic experience.

2. Ethical

   The ethical area is concerned with principles underlying practical morality, descriptions of right and wrong conduct, obligations, duties and rights.

3. Linguistic

   The linguistic area is concerned with the use of words in listening and reading, talking and writing. These activities help the individual to receive and process information, to enter the world of ideas, to make sense of these experiences, and to relate to others.

4. Mathematical

   The mathematical area is concerned with familiarity with numbers and symbols and the ability to use them with confidence. It includes communicating, problem solving and generalising. Communicating means transmitting and interpreting information conveyed by tables, diagrams and models. Problem solving involves identifying the variables in a real problem, setting up an abstract model of the problem and using mathematical techniques to solve it. Generalising implies seeking and recognising patterns and relationships and justifying conclusions by a logical argument expressed in precise, unambiguous language.

5. Physical

The physical area is concerned with awareness and understanding of the human body. It involves movement, through the development and maintenance of bodily skills, co-ordination and control, and manipulative abilities. Such experience of movement leads to an understanding of the spatial dimensions and an appreciation of natural forces. Movement is a means of non-verbal communication in which the individual may respond to a stimulus drawing upon past experience and imagination.

6. Scientific

The scientific area is concerned especially with observing, predicting and experimenting. Observing requires direct or indirect evidence from the physical world. Predicting will be based consciously or unconsciously on a hypothesis which explains patterns of previous observation. Predicting shows what will be the next most significant observation and its testing may require experimenting, the use of apparatus, physical skills, measurement and calculation. Observing, predicting and experimenting do not merely make up the organised knowledge of the natural world which is called science; they constitute a powerful method of problem solving.

7. Social/Political

The social and political area is concerned with relationships within society; between individuals and social groups and between social groups. It involves consideration of beliefs and values, of purposes and motivation, of rules and conventions, of authority and power.

Understanding one's own personal relationships requires self-knowledge as well as knowledge of and sensitivity towards others.

8. Spiritual

The spiritual area is concerned with the awareness a person has of those elements in existence and experience which may be defined in terms of inner feelings and beliefs; they affect the way people see themselves and throw light for them on the purpose and meaning of life itself. Often these feelings and beliefs lead people to claim to know God and to glimpse the transcendent: sometimes they represent that striving and longing for perfection which characterises human beings but always they are concerned with matters at the heart and root of existence.

The spiritual area is concerned with everything in human knowledge or experience that is connected with or derived from a sense of God or of Gods. Spiritual is a meaningless adjective for the atheist and of dubious use to the agnostic. Irrespective of personal belief or disbelief an unaccountable number of people have believed and do believe in the spiritual aspects of human life, and, therefore, their actions, attitude and interpretations of events have been influenced accordingly.

General Principles of Curriculum Design

In addition to guaranteeing to all pupils access to these areas of experience the curriculum of each school is designed to ensure that

1. all pupils are educated according to their age and aptitudes and to the fullest extent of their abilities;

127

2. the needs of those who learn slowly and with difficulty are met as an integral part of the school's provision;

3. as far as possible learning is rooted in the pupils' personal experience and relates to practical everyday needs;

4. there is equality of opportunity between both sexes at all stages;

5. full account is taken of the need to educate all children to take their place in a society which is multi-cultural and multi-ethnic;

6. each stage of education follows easily, naturally and effectively from the one which has gone before and forms a firm basis for the next.

The Curriculum at Different Stages of Education

The Primary Stage 5-11

The purpose of the curriculum followed by the youngest children in each school is to introduce them to the widest possible range of experiences which will extend their understanding of the world in which they live and enable them to acquire and develop the attitudes, values, ideas and skills which will form a sound basis for secondary school and eventually for adult life.

Younger children do not compartmentalize knowledge into separate subjects. Often a single activity promotes a variety of skills. In the primary school therefore one teacher is usually responsible for the entire work of one class. This enables skills to be to be applied and practised in a variety of situations. At the upper end of the primary school however some activities will be presented as separate subjects to those children who are ready for this approach.

The Secondary Stage 11-16

The curriculum of the secondary school is likely to be organised in terms of separate subject areas even in the first three years when most pupils follow the same broadly based course of studies before they are required to specialise in subjects for vocational and examination purposes.

For this reason the remainder of the paper is largely expressed in terms of traditional subject areas, although it must be borne constantly in mind that they are only means towards the wider educational aims which have been set out and that, even within their own terms, they overlap and are heavily dependent on each other, hence a degree of unavoidable repetition. This is immediately apparent in the following description of a number of areas which are brought together in curricular planning for particular attention under the heading "Preparation for Adult Life", although they are all separately represented in the subject areas which are described in greater detail later.

PREPARATION FOR ADULT LIFE

All school experience is, of course, a preparation for adult life in one way or another. This particular phrase has, however, taken on a narrower and more specific meaning for secondary schools, namely the deliberate steps which need to be taken, and which are not possible through traditional subject areas alone, to prepare young people successfully for adult life through their personal and social development and through political education in its broadest sense, that is the knowledge and skills needed to live in society and contribute to it.

All secondary schools, therefore, offer a considered programme of personal and social development and political education both as a separate constituent of the timetable and as a dimension of the curriculum as a whole, in which particular attention is paid to the following

(a) the importance and development of high moral standards in behaviour, principles and outlook and of personal qualities of good character;

(b) the importance and development of good personal relationships; a knowledge of the nature of the individual and of oneself; self-reliance, the ability to take responsibility for one's own actions;

team work, the possession of a sense of belonging and commitment to a group;

(c) the development of those qualities, particularly of inventiveness, curiosity and imagination, which make the greatest contribution to self-fulfilment and recreation and the best use of leisure time;

(d) the ability to look after one's health; a knowledge of elementary considerations of safety and the principles of first aid; an understanding of common infectious diseases and of the effects of alcohol, drugs and tobacco; a knowledge of health and welfare agencies and of how to use them;

(e) an awareness of the responsibilities of parenthood; an understanding of the bodily and emotional changes from childhood through adolescence to adulthood; a knowledge of the factors involved in human reproduction and in the development of the child from conception to infancy, an awareness of the needs of young children; a knowledge of the skills and values which go into making a good home;

(f) the development of social awareness through a feeling of mutual obligation and sensitivity to the needs of others, especially minorities and the disadvantaged; an understanding of the needs and problems of the community; an awareness of the knowledge, values, attitudes and skills needed to protect and improve the environment;

(g) a knowledge and understanding of how major political decisions are made and who makes them; the machinery of international, central and local Government; the political parties; a working grasp of major political concepts and knowledge of specific issues; an ability to understand the political interests and views of others;

(h) a knowledge of basic legal rights and duties, of who makes the law and how it is administered, of sources of legal information and advice;

(i) a knowledge and understanding of the national economy and how resources are distributed, of the place of Great Britain as a manufacturing commercial and agricultural nation within the world economy; a working grasp of major economic concepts enabling judgements to be made; a knowledge of matters affecting personal and family finance and housekeeping and consumer protection;

(j) a realistic idea of what paid employment means; an awareness of the essential requirements for employment, principally educational qualifications and personal qualities; a knowledge of training, further education and employment opportunities, sources of help and information; procedures for finding work.

As part of this programme all schools encourage involvement in voluntary, community and charitable activities and participation in extra curricular activities. All pupils have an opportunity to take part in debates and discussions on issues of the day and in decisions affecting aspects of their school life and in programmes of work experience.

Central to the personal and social development of every pupil and to the curriculum as a whole is the moral and religious education offered in all schools.

RELIGIOUS EDUCATION

The law requires that Religious Education is taught to all children through a syllabus agreed with teachers and local Christian denominations. The aims given below are taken from the Agreed Syllabus followed in Croydon's schools.

All pupils by the time they leave primary school should

(a) have experience and have been led to an awareness of aspects of the natural world which evoke awe and wonder, leading towards a conception of a caring God;

(b) have developed some capacity to communicate these experiences;

(c) have begun to develop the capacity to form relationships based on love, sympathy and consideration;

(d) have begun to enter imaginatively and with sensitivity into other people's experiences, e.g. happiness, loneliness and sickness;

(e) know something of the ways in which people express and have expressed their religious experiences and have a glimpse of the significance of these experiences.

During their time at secondary school all pupils should

(a) come to have a knowledge of the Christian religion, its faith, worship, origins and beliefs;

(b) be aware of other religions and faiths;

(c) acquire an appreciation that many people, famous and little known, find and have found inspiration for living and strength through their religious faith;

(d) become aware that personal religious belief shapes a person's attitudes which are reflected in day-to-day behaviour in the community.

Before they leave secondary schools all pupils should

(a) broaden and deepen their knowledge and understanding of the Christian Faith and of other religions and philosophies;

(b) investigate the nature of morality and experience the making of moral decisions and appreciate that such decisions have their basis in belief and values;

(c) acquire skills, whereby some evaluation of the claims religion and philosophy make may be undertaken;

(d) develop an awareness of the part that religion can play in their own lives as a vital element of human experience.

ENGLISH AND MATHEMATICS

It is clearly of the greatest importance that all pupils when they leave school at 16 should have as great a command of English and Mathematics as their abilities will permit. For this reason these two subjects are taught throughout the years of compulsory education from 5-16, and a responsibility is placed on all teachers, not only those who specialise in English or Mathematics, to use their teaching to improve general standards of literacy and numeracy at every opportunity.

The two subjects, however, differ in three important respects. First, English does not hold together as a body of knowledge which can be identified, quantified, and then transmitted in the same way as much of Mathematics can be defined and used. Second, whereas progress in Mathematics very often depends on a sufficient understanding of one or more pieces of work which have gone before, competence in language is achieved as a pattern of experience formed through the interaction of talking, listening, reading and writing. Third, performance in language depends to a far greater degree on a pupil's maturity and personal experience than Mathematics where high levels of attainment can be reached at a very young age.

For these reasons, although English and Mathematics share the same central importance in the curriculum, the programme of work described in the following chapters relating to each of them shows marked differences.

AIMS OF ENGLISH 5-16

It is one of the Education Committee's main aims that all pupils leaving school at 16 will be able to use the English language confidently, appropriately and accurately, to the best of their ability. They should be able to speak their own mind, to write what they have thought and to have a care for the correctness of written and spoken English. They should be able to understand what they read and hear, to master ideas and restate them in their own way. They should have some understanding of the different uses of language, of the language which narrates, describes, evokes, persuades and is the instrument of the creative imagination.

Language is, primarily, a means of communication and of learning by representing the world to ourselves by means of generalisation and by reducing complexity to simple issues. Progress is to be measured by the degree to which pupils come to exercise, as they get older, a greater command over matters requiring abstraction and complexity through the development of the basic skills acquired in earlier years: one cannot with precision, therefore, speak of different kinds of language ability belonging to different chronological ages or stages of development.

For this reason every primary and secondary school regards the language development of its pupils as a continuous process involving talking and listening, reading and writing, in which all teachers have a part to play, and each school has specific written policies to see that this continuity and community of effort is achieved.

The purpose of teaching the English language in primary and secondary schools is to ensure that all pupils

    (a) principally through talking and listening:

        (i)   develop receptive skills, in particular the ability to listen attentively and with understanding, appropriate to different purposes and situations;

        (ii)   learn to convey meaning, to increase their knowledge and understanding appropriate to different purposes and in a variety of contexts;

        (iii) develop the ability to talk confidently, to share and analyse meanings and feelings;

        (iv) develop the ability to use language as an instrument of thought, to be analytical, to consider alternatives, to process new ideas and concepts and to apply them in other contexts;

(v)   develop and encourage the ability to question;

(vi) are able to follow the line of and contribute appropriately to an argument or sustained discussion;

(vii) develop through drama opportunities for learning by talk, movement and interaction with others;

(b) through reading

(i)   are able to read silently or aloud with fluency, accuracy, understanding and, above all, for enjoyment;

(ii)   gain an understanding of the concept of story and of the fundamental differences between spoken and written language;

(iii) develop a discriminating and critical attitude towards what is read, and the ability to select and evaluate material;

(iv)   develop an understanding and appreciation of the ways writers achieve their effects, and are able to recognise underlying meaning and perceive attitudes, tone, mood and style;

(v)   develop the habit of reading for pleasure in and out of school for sustained periods and gain an enjoyment of literature and a love of words;

(vi)   develop and extend the notion of reading for learning so that books and other reference materials are used effectively to gain knowledge;

(vii) develop strategies such as skimming, scanning and interpretation;

(viii) gain concepts of how other people think and feel by experiencing through prose and poetry not only a variety of literary forms, styles and approaches but also a variety of literary heritages and cultures;

(c) through writing

   (i)   learn how to express meaning clearly, fluently and in logical sequence appropriate to different purposes and audiences and for a variety of occasions;

   (ii)   develop a legible style of handwriting and understand the importance of neat and appropriate presentation;

   (iii)   develop the confidence to explore their thoughts, feelings and ideas through prose, poetry and drama;

   (iv)   develop technical accuracy in terms of grammar, syntax, punctuation and spelling;

   (v)   develop a variety of ways of recording information and findings including note-taking and summary.

Primary School 5-11

It is the main purpose of teaching at the infant stage between the ages of 5 and 8 to ensure that the foundations of listening, talking, reading and writing are thoroughly laid and that pupils acquire the basic skills they will need in mature reading and writing later on: in particular a knowledge of the alphabet and the relationship between letters and sounds, the ability to group letters into simple words and words into simple sentences, the ability to begin to read and write with accuracy, fluency and understanding.

The junior school will build on the work of the infant school. In particular it will encourage the growth of vocabulary and extend the understanding and use of word and sentence structure and spelling patterns. Additional resources will be provided where a child does not show an expected ability to make meaning out of words in context, in short, where the beginnings of fluency in reading and writing with understanding are absent.

Secondary School 11-16

By the age of 11 all pupils should be able to read with enjoyment and understanding and to begin to derive an author's implied as well as explicit meaning. At this age also pupils should be able to look more critically at written style and to express their main thoughts in their own language.

Similarly, in writing, pupils will have had the experience of using the basic styles of describing, narrating and explaining etc., bearing in mind various different audiences.

The secondary school will build on this junior school foundation, taking into consideration the language needs and abilities of individual pupils.

The basic styles of writing, mentioned above as objectives at the age of 11, will be further developed, so that skills are obtained, for example, to write letters, to create a dialogue, to take notes, to make a summary, to construct an argument and, at times, to write intensively in verse.

From the literary point of view attention will be paid to well known stories, poems and plays by contemporary and modern 20th century writers. A balance will be drawn between a study of these and of great authors of the past. Levels of sophistication will determine which age groups and which classes carry out such studies and when.

Under-pinning everything will be a careful development of the technical side of language which manifests itself largely in competence in written work.

All pupils do not achieve an easy mastery of grammar, but instruction will be given in the basic forms of sentence, i.e. statement, question and command, both simple and complex, and in all appropriate aspects of parts of speech, vocabulary work, spelling and punctuation.

Much good English teaching and learning is encapsulated in comprehension exercises. These combine the skills of reading, thinking and writing, and, when carefully compiled and administered, assist pupils in establishing how far their achievement in English has progressed.

ASSESSMENT IN ENGLISH

All pupils will be regularly assessed by the teachers to ensure that they are progressing to the best of their ability. It is important to realise, however, that because children develop at widely differing rates, it is not possible to make any overall statement about specific language skills which should be mastered at specific ages.

It is however possible to point to certain goals in reading and writing, which the majority of pupils should have reached.

At 8 pupils should be able to read simple, continuous prose and poetry with understanding and enjoyment. They should be able to write accurately in simple sentences and to use the appropriate punctuation such as full-stops or question marks.

At 11 pupils should be able to read more complicated materials, both fiction and non-fiction, to assist their learning across the various curriculum subjects. Furthermore they should be able to write confidently in more complex sentences, for a greater variety of purposes, and with a growing understanding of punctuation and paragraphing.

At 14 a pupil's reading skill should allow a study of a variety of texts and at various levels of comprehension. Equally, in writing, pupils should be able to produce accurate, clear, but not necessarily complicated, continuous prose which reflects a more adult approach to thought and language. Good presentation and handwriting should be expected in all finished writing.

A Borough-wide continuous assessment of the performance of all pupils in comprehension and writing takes place and parents will be informed of their children's development.

In addition, all pupils are given a standardised reading test at 7, 11 and 14 in order to relate individual performance in reading to the average level of performance of children of the same age. Those pupils whose reading age falls below their developmental age will be given additional help.

All pupils in their later years of secondary schooling will, according to their ability, be prepared for public examination in English for the General Certificate of Education at '0' level, the Certificate of Secondary Education or papers set by the Royal Society of Arts and the City and Guilds Boards.

AIMS OF MATHEMATICAL EDUCATION 5-16

It is one of the Education Committee's main aims that all pupils leaving school at 16 will be able to use, effectively and with confidence, the mathematical skills and understanding they will need for adult life, employment, further study and training; in particular that they will have a feeling for number and measurement which enables suitable estimation and approximation and straightforward mental calculation to be made.

It is also intended that the personal development of every pupil should be enhanced through the particular reliance the teaching of Mathematics places on neatness, accuracy, logical thinking, precise and concise expression and perseverance in solving problems, and that all pupils will develop an appreciation and enjoyment of Mathematics for its own sake, a realization of its role in the development of Science and Technology and our civilization and an awareness of its value as a powerful means of communication.

THE CURRICULUM

In the teaching of Mathematics between the years 5-16 emphasis will be laid at all stages on the practical application of basic mathematical skills and knowledge to everyday experience outside the classroom. Pupils will be taught to use a variety of measuring and drawing instruments and will become familiar with both the commonly used metric and Imperial units of measurement.

Donald Naismith

Primary School 5-11

Primary education, covering infant and junior schooling, is an important time when the foundations of later work are laid and attitudes to Mathematics are formed.

In the infant stage between the ages of 5 and 8 children will be introduced to a variety of basic mathematical concepts in a way which builds upon their experiences and clearly links Mathematics to the physical world. Work in Mathematics and language are closely related and pupils will be encouraged to express their mathematical thinking orally and in writing. Care will be taken to develop links between everyday language and Mathematics before children are taught either technical terms or symbols and to ensure that children are not asked to perform formal operations on abstract quantities before they have learned even the simplest number concepts. A summary of the Mathematics which will be taught to all pupils at this stage is given in Appendix 1.

Between the ages of 8 and 11 the junior school will develop the work started in the infant school. The ground to be covered at this stage is given as Appendix 2. Its scope is deliberately less than that often seen in primary textbooks to ensure that the progress of those pupils who have difficulty with mathematical ideas will not suffer from their attempting an overcrowded syllabus. Those pupils, however, who clearly show mathematical ability of a high order at this stage will be encouraged to make and test their own generalisations from their own practical and mathematical experience. They will also be given opportunities to develop strategic, analytical and abstract skills by applying their existing skills and knowledge to practical and unfamiliar problems.

The work with simple electronic calculators is not intended to reduce the pupils' ability to perform simple calculations mentally or on paper, but to aid understanding, particularly of decimals, and to facilitate work with more detailed and extended problems through removing unnecessary stages of mechanical calculation.

Secondary School 11-16

This is the first experience which pupils have of being taught by specialist mathematics teachers whose first duty with the younger pupils is to ensure that any deficiencies in mathematical knowledge or skills are remedied.

All pupils will study Mathematics throughout this period of their education. The minimum ground they will cover is outlined in Appendix 3A although many pupils will achieve much more, as outlined in Appendix 3B.

It is important to understand that there is no clear cut distinction between Modern and Traditional Mathematics as they are not alternative bodies of knowledge. All pupils will follow courses which embody the best of both approaches while avoiding the excesses of each.

It is also important to realise that Mathematics is a subject for which people display greatly varying aptitudes. For this reason different courses of study will be followed by pupils of different ability.

Pupils for whom the G.C.E. and C.S.E. examination are not appropriate will follow a course based on the Foundation Curriculum defined in the Cockcroft Report and outlined in Appendix 3A. Wherever possible, more able pupils mathematically will follow an extension of the ordinary syllabus involving greater pace, wider outlook and variety of application, a broader opportunity to extend investigations of topics which catch the imagination and encouragement to undertake supplementary reading.

Statistics will be an essential part of the Mathematics studied by all pupils and will be offered as an examination subject.

TEACHING ARRANGEMENTS

All pupils will study Mathematics from 5-16. In primary schools pupils are taught Mathematics everyday within a total time allocation of between 4 and 5 hours a week. In secondary schools the time allocation will vary between 2½ and 3½ hours a week. All examination classes are taught in groups differentiated by ability, although some classes unavoidably have groups of pupils attempting different examinations. Pupils of exceptional mathematical ability have additional mathematical activities provided both by their school and by the Education Authority.

Mathematics teaching at all levels will include opportunities for

(i)   exposition by the teacher,

(ii)   discussion between teacher and pupils and between pupils themselves;

(iii) appropriate practical work;

(iv) consolidation and practice of fundamental skills and routines;

(v)   problem solving, including the application of Mathematics to everyday situations;

(vi) investigational work.

Importance will be attached to mental Mathematics, the habit of solving problems presented orally, and pupils will be encouraged to make use of whatever method of mental calculations suits them best.

ASSESSMENT IN MATHEMATICS

All pupils will be regularly assessed by their teachers to ensure that they are developing to the best of their ability. At 7, 11 and 14, a Borough-wide assessment of the performance of all pupils takes place and parents will be informed of their children's results. The levels of competence which should be reached by most children during the stages of their education are given in the appendices, although it will be recognised that individually children develop at widely differing rates.

All pupils in the later years of secondary schooling will be prepared for public examination in Mathematics or in Numeracy.

Pupils who are not entered for either the G.C.E. or C.S.E. examination will be prepared for examinations in Numeracy by taking one of the following courses:

The Associated Examining Board's Certificate of Proficiency in Arithmetic or Basic Maths; the City and Guilds Certificate of Numeracy or the Royal Society of Arts School Leaver's Attainment Profile of Numerical Skills.

THE ARTS

Although a command of English and Mathematics - literacy and numeracy - are necessary means of communication for all children, many if not most will find their most powerful means of self-expression through the Arts, through art, music, drama and physical activity. They are essential to the personal development of all pupils, in particular their creativity, individuality and self-awareness, their sense of purpose and fulfilment, their ability to discriminate and make judgments and their capacity for personal commitment, effort and enjoyment. In addition music, drama and physical activity provide the opportunity for team work necessary for other qualities such as leadership and an awareness of the contribution each can bring to co-operative effort.

For these reasons art, music, drama and physical activity all form part of the experience of all children throughout their time at primary and secondary school with the following aims.

ART

All pupils should by the time they leave secondary school, through their study of art and design, be able to take pleasure in creation, have enough skill to be successful in their chosen media and have confidence to communicate visually without inhibition. They should have acquired the ability to observe and analyse and express what they see with feeling, understanding and discrimination, a sharpened inventiveness and a critical awareness of aesthetic values and commercial influences. They should be able to talk about their art and that of other people.

All pupils will at all stages of their education follow programmes involving practical experience of all the major areas of artistic study and practice; drawing, painting, printmaking and three-dimensional work calling for visual, tactile and intellectual judgments as well as emotional responses through a heightened awareness of shape, colour, texture and all those elements which form a visual vocabulary.

Pupils will have opportunities to follow courses leading to the General Certificate of Education and the Certificate of Secondary Education.

MUSIC

All pupils at the end of their time at Secondary School should have developed in varying degrees most of the following: a critical and sensitive response to sound of all kinds, the ability to listen receptively to a wide range of music, some facility in using voices and instruments individually or in groups as a medium for personal expression, and some skills in using musical notation. Classroom music aims to provide pupils with both the knowledge and the skills necessary to enable them to gain greater enjoyment from listening to or taking part in musical performance.

In Primary Schools emphasis will be placed on acquiring, through practical activity, the following basic skills: to listen carefully, to sing in tune, to keep in time, to respond through movement, to imitate and invent rhythms and melodies, to read simple passages of music, to play by ear simple melodies on pitched percussion or other instruments, to recognise and identify pitch, rhythm, timbre and tempo, to develop a musical memory. All pupils will have the opportunity to make their own music both individually and with others. Pupils will also be assisted in listening with understanding to a variety of musical styles of different cultural heritages.

In Secondary Schools all pupils will be encouraged to develop the skills and build on the knowledge they acquired during Primary School, to familiarise themselves with and learn to appreciate critically a diversity of musical idioms, and to widen their musical experience generally. Opportunity will be provided for those pupils who wish to follow courses leading to the General Certificate of education and the Certificate of Secondary Education.

Pupils of both junior and secondary age range who display an ability in classroom music-making will be given the opportunity of receiving specialist instrumental tuition and will be encouraged to play in ensembles and orchestras, both in school and at the Borough's Organised Centres.

All pupils will be encouraged to join in as wide a range of extra-curricular activities as possible. Besides the musical expertise and enjoyment gained, taking part in any musical performance is a unique experience which generates team spirit and develops sensitivity within an individual.

DRAMA

The importance of drama lies in its unique capacity to develop essential bodily skills with the faculty of speech, whilst at the same time providing a means of exploring social attitudes, personal relationships, hopes and inner conflict.

In the earliest years of primary school it will be indistinguishable from play. Later two separate but related strands will appear: theatre, offering experience in the use of recognised dramatic and technical skills in improvisation and scripted plays; and, educational drama involving learning through simulated role play.

In secondary school a more critical and structured approach will be developed and the range of subject matter and its treatment extended. Study of theatre and educational drama will continue to be important. All pupils who show particular talent and interest in drama will have the opportunity to involve themselves in the staging of dramatic events and in the observation of theatrical performances and, where appropriate, to follow courses leading to the General Certificate of Education and the Certificate of Secondary Education.

At the end of their time at secondary school, it is intended that all pupils will, through their study of drama, have gained confidence in movement and speaking and an inventiveness in acting, have experienced joining in a major theatrical event and have had the opportunity of enjoying plays and good theatre. They will have a knowledge of period and authors and will have acquired a critical sense. In particular it is hoped that they will have a sensitivity to and sympathy with people in other walks of life and predicaments and in other places and an awareness of moral and social issues.

PHYSICAL ACTIVITIES

The essential aim of Physical Education in schools is to develop, through the purposeful experience of movement, physical skills and qualities of character which encourage participation and involvement in worthwhile physical activities throughout life, and which make an important contribution to the pupil's enjoyment and personal development generally. Particular attention will be paid to the development of strength, stamina, skill and co-ordination, qualities of leadership, initiative, co-operation, self-reliance and high standards of personal behaviour. All pupils at all stages of their education will follow a balanced and progressive programme in a range of activities appropriate to their age and physical development in which Athletics, Dance, Games, Gymnastics, Swimming and Outdoor Activities will be essential elements.

Opportunities will be afforded to all pupils to take part in individual and team activities and competition, and to measure their personal attainments through taking part in graded tests, and, in competition against others, in inter-group, school, district and national events.

Aesthetic experience in the appreciation of form, rhythm and spatial relationships will be provided principally through Gymnastics and Dance, involving an introduction to a variety of styles and opportunities to meet the needs of those who show interest and talent in specialised forms.

It is intended that all pupils before they leave primary school will have the opportunity to learn to swim and have been introduced before they leave secondary school to water safety and life-saving techniques.

Pupils will have the opportunity to take part in various outdoor education activities, such as rock-climbing, canoeing, sailing and camping.

Health and fitness will be integral to the Physical Education Programme and taught in a structured and identifiable way. Emphasis will be placed on the structure and working of the human body to develop an understanding of the scientific and mechanical principles in practical activities, bodily care and physical well-being.

Pupils will be prepared and encouraged to join clubs and teams when they leave school.

Particular attention will be paid to the needs of those pupils who find it hard to take part in, enjoy and succeed in physical activities. In addition, opportunities will also be afforded for those pupils with particular talents to develop their skills.

HUMANITIES

The term Humanities covers those subject areas which have to do with man in time in place and in society and which are usually referred to separately as History, Geography, and Social Studies which in turn encompasses Economics, Sociology, and Government and Politics. Religious Education is often included in this grouping.

The study of Humanities makes a major contribution to three important underlying educational aims:-

to help pupils to appreciate human institutions and aspirations; to instil respect for religious and moral values and tolerance of other races, religions and ways of life; and to help pupils to understand the world in which they live and the interdependence of individuals, groups and nations.

As such Humanities occupies a central position in the programme of work followed by all pupils throughout their time in primary and secondary schools and has among its chief aims that all pupils should develop:

    (a) The skills needed to <u>find out</u> information by deciding on the type of facts required, by locating appropriate sources of information, and by extracting the relevant material from text, statistics, maps, pictures, people, objects and places;

(b) The skill to <u>think clearly</u> about evidence, in evaluating it, in distinguishing between fact and assertion, in detecting bias, in analysing, in forming judgments and in making decisions;

(c) <u>Responsible attitudes and values</u> in respect of truth and untruth, accuracy and inaccuracy, tolerance and intolerance, right and wrong, dependence and interdependence, aspiration and achievement and rights and responsibilities.

<u>Primary School 5-11</u>

All pupils throughout their time in primary school will follow a balanced programme of work drawn from History, Geography, and Social Studies. Much of the work at this stage will be approached in an integrated manner, and it will often be difficult to fix convenient labels to the activities taking place.

All pupils leaving primary school at 11 should have, through their study of <u>History</u>,

(a) heard well-told stories about the past designed to stimulate their imagination and to create and reinforce a desire to know more;

(b) been introduced to a time scale;

(c) found out and presented evidence about people and events within their own life times;

(d) studied the immediate vicinity of the school (or other localities) from an historical point of view using both fieldwork techniques and appropriate secondary sources;

(e) had experience of using as wide a range as possible of both primary and secondary sources, enabling them to make sense of a secondary school course.

All pupils leaving primary schools at 11 should have, through their study of <u>Geography</u>,

    (a) experienced the drawing of plans and maps from direct observation and measurement sufficiently often to be able to carry out basic mapping tasks including the use of simple scales, mapping symbols and co-ordinates and experienced using a compass and done sufficient associated tasks to be able to use the eight points of the compass with confidence;

    (b) studied the immediate vicinity of the school (or other localities) from a Geographical point of view, making measurements and observations and recording them and using appropriate secondary sources;

    (c) undertaken basic observation and recording of the weather.

    (d) acquired a general knowledge of the universe, the solar system and the structure of the earth;

    (e) become familiar with the major land masses and oceans of the world through substantial experience of using a simple atlas and a globe;

    (f) become familiar with a map of Great Britain and acquired some knowledge of the major British regions and cities;

    (g) been introduced to differing life styles in some other countries.

All pupils leaving primary school at 11 should, through their <u>Social Studies</u>, have developed some understanding of their local community and of ways of finding out about it, based on practical experience.

<u>The Secondary School 11-16</u>

All pupils will continue their study of History and Geography and Social Studies throughout their time in secondary school at the end of which all students at 16 will

Through their study of History

(a) have had experience of using evidence in History (including fieldwork and Museum visits) so as to be able to comment historically;

(b) understand and be able to give examples illustrating the basic concepts of change and continuity, time and period, cause and effect, historical uncertainty and interdependence;

(c) have been encouraged to develop a sympathetic understanding of particular periods, personalities and events;

(d) have sufficient knowledge of the political, social economic and cultural background to the modern world to be able to relate major items of world news to a wider context;

(e) have sufficient knowledge and understanding of British History including the modern period, to be able to comment sensibly on the Historical dimension of national events and to be aware of the cultural, economic, political and social heritage we possess.

Through their study of Geography

(a) have had experience of using maps, including ordnance survey maps of different scales and be able to plan a route between two places on the same map.

(b) understand and be able to give examples illustrating the basic concepts involved in agricultural and industrial location and production, settlement patterns, communications, climate, and the shaping of the landscape by man and by nature;

(c) have sufficient knowledge of the major political, economic, physical and climatic regions of the world to be able to relate major items of world news to a wider context;

(d) have sufficient knowledge of the human and physical Geography of Great Britain to be able, for example, to plan a journey or a holiday sensibly;

(e) have had sufficient experience of geographical fieldwork to be able to comment on salient geographical features in the local environment and in wider rural and urban environments.

Through their Social Studies

(a) have studied the democratic process locally and nationally and have taken part in a range of structured democratic decision making processes;

(b) have studied the wealth creating process nationally and internationally, and be aware of the major factors resulting in relative wealth and poverty;

(c) have studied the various patterns of social interaction common in this country, and be aware of the effects of differing attitudes and behaviour;

(d) understand and be able to give examples illustrating the basic concepts of power and influence, conformity and deviance, dependence and independence, and stereotyping;

(e) be able to talk sensibly about a range of the most significant economic, political, and social issues confronting the country and the world.

(f) be aware of the major personal decisions to be made in the years after 16 and have knowledge and understanding of the types of information needed if the best possible decisions are to be made and of how such information can be acquired.

All pupils will have the opportunity to follow as far as their abilities will allow courses in History and Geography leading to the General Certificate of Education and the Certificate of Secondary Education, and at least one subject drawn from Social Studies, Religious Education, Economics, Sociology, Government and Politics.

FOREIGN LANGUAGES

European Modern Languages

The Education Committee agrees with the view that 'although English has established a dominant position as an international language, experience indicates that individual countries will continue to assert the importance of their language as a reflection of their national identity' and that 'in respecting and responding to that situation it is important that we re-affirm our commitment to foreign language learning rather than being encouraged to accept the illusory view that a knowledge of English will suffice'.

It is, therefore, the aim of the Education Committee that young people leaving school have as great a command of at least one foreign language as possible and have developed their linguistic competence to its fullest extent.

For this reason all pupils whatever their background are offered a common experience of learning a European modern language which is foreign to them, and in the first three years of secondary school follow a carefully structured scheme along the lines described on the following page.

All schools offer at least two European foreign languages for those pupils who are capable of success in public examination at the end of their secondary education. Candidates are entered for the G.C.E. and the C.S.E. examinations.

Foreign language teaching is not undertaken in primary schools.

Bi-Lingual Pupils

Where there are sufficient numbers, pupils for whom English is their second language may be prepared for public examination in their first language. Where there are insufficient numbers to justify timetabled provision of this kind, pupils shall be entered for public examination in their first language individually.

The Classical Languages: Latin and Greek

The study of the Latin and Greek languages is not offered in secondary schools, although the opportunity exists for it to be undertaken after the age of 16.

A knowledge and understanding of the culture, the social and political development and the philosophical, scientific and aesthetic achievements of the Greco-Roman world are, however, essential elements of the curriculum followed in all schools.

Donald Naismith

OUTLINE OF POSSIBLE LINGUISTIC GOALS FOR PUPILS STUDYING A FIRST FOREIGN LANGUAGE FROM THE AGE OF ELEVEN

	Goals for pupils likely to terminate their study after				Goals for those completing a 5 year course	
	3 years		3, 4, or 5 years depending on local circumstances and on motivation	Goals after 3 years of study for abler pupils likely to complete a 5 year course		
LISTENING	Understanding of concrete everyday language used in specified situations; ability to identify subject matter of speech so as to respond in English or by action.	Understanding of concrete language within wider range of lexis and structures.	Understanding of everyday language in an increasing range of situations.	Greater understanding of everyday language spoken at near normal speed.	Detailed understanding of concrete language spoken by a native at near normal speed and involving familiar language; gist understanding of language similarly spoken over wider range of lexis structures.	Detailed understanding of language spoken by a native at near normal speed within areas of language already encountered but includes abstract forms; gist understanding of language containing some unfamiliar lexis

READING	Recognition reading of a simple routine nature: shop signs, labels, products, signs, etc.	Wider range of vocabulary and structures: gist reading of a more consecutive nature	Understanding of simple items such as letters, notices and short narrative texts.	Detailed reading of items such as letters, notices and simple foreign texts; gist understanding of a wider range of reading materials.	Detailed and gist understanding of concrete language in newspapers, advertisements, formal and informal letters and possibly adapted foreign texts.	Detailed and gist understanding of fiction and of non-fiction studied intensively or extensively.
SPEAKING	Two-language communication with each speaker using his own language.	The ability to ask for simple information in the foreign language; further speech in English.	The ability to ask and answer specified questions satisfying simple routine needs and minimum courtesy requirements.	The ability to ask and answer questions concerning everyday needs and including simple narrative and description (in tenses other than the present.)	The ability to ask and answer questions in a wider variety of situations and involving increasing complexity of structure and breadth of vocabulary.	Relatively fluent, flexible and accurate use of language; some measure of confidence in initiating language and in expressing interests, feelings and ideas.
WRITING	Significant as a goal only as an aid to memory and to help to give pupils a sense of achievement.		Reproduction of Language encountered in speech (above); very simple letter-writing.	Writing of dialogue, narrative and simple letters of a personal type.	Personal writing about about family, home and interests; letters and simple compositions.	Relatively accurate and fluent personal writing about family, home and interest as well as narrative and descriptive composition.
	Least able pupils	Below average pupils	Pupils of average ability	Able pupils		Very able pupils

AIMS OF SCIENCE EDUCATION 5-16

It is the Education Committee's policy that Science should form part of the experience of every pupil throughout his time at primary and secondary school with the following aims:

(a) to equip all pupils with a broadly based scientific knowledge leading to a better understanding of themselves and the world and to an awareness of man's scientific and technological background and achievements and their ever increasing effects on his everyday life.

(b) to develop personal qualities of curiosity, enquiry, and original thought and practical skills and attitudes needed in a fast changing world, especially those required for employment and, in particular, observation, recording, communication, pattern recognition, theoretical modelling, evaluation and analysis,

and

(c) to provide opportunities to experience the pleasure, fascination and enthusiasm to be derived from scientific discovery and the appreciation of scientific facts and concepts and to take part in practical experimentation and investigation, either individually or as part of a team.

THE CURRICULUM

Primary School 5-11

The aims of Primary School Science are to develop in all pupils an enquiring mind and a scientific approach to problems through the following broad approaches

1. Developing Attitudes, Interests and Aesthetic Awareness:

willingness to answer questions, to handle both living and non-living material; sensitivity to the needs of living things; enjoyment in using all the senses for exploring and discriminating; willingness to collect material for observation and investigation.

2. Encouragement of Observing, Exploration and Ordering Observations:

appreciation of the variety of living things and materials in the environment; awareness of changes which take place as time passes; recognition of common shapes - square, circle, triangle; extension work with rectangles and hexagons; recognition of common shapes in the environment, of regularity in patterns: ability to group things consistently according to chosen or given criteria.

3. Posing Questions and Devising Experiments or Investigations to Answer Them:

ability to find answers to simple problems by investigation, and to make comparisons in terms of one property or variable.

4. Acquiring Knowledge and Learning Skills:

ability to discriminate between different materials; awareness of the characteristics of living things; and of the properties which materials have; ability to use reference material.

5. Communications:

ability to use new words appropriately, to record events in their proper sequence, to discuss and record impressions of living and non-living things in the environment, to use representational symbols for recording information on charts or block graphs.

6. Appreciation Patterns and Relationships:

awareness of cause/effect relationships.

7.   <u>Interpreting Findings Critically</u>:

   awareness that the apparent size, shape and relationships of things depends on the position of the observer.

In the infant stage emphasis will be placed on the processes of Science. Much scientific work will be indistinguishable from other activities, in particular Mathematics at this level where the concepts of length, mass/weight, volume/capacity and time are formulated and developed by practical experience. Science work will also lend itself to ready expression in Art and Craft and will play a major role in language development. In spite of this Science will be approached as a separate discipline and schemes of work will depend on content as well as method.

The junior school will build on the progress of the infant school. Objectives will become more sharply focussed and more specific emphasis placed on those scientific processes using symbolic representation, apparatus, and/or measuring instruments and observation and involving interpretation and application, and the design and performance of investigations. In all cases the work followed will be based on specific materials and phenomena and the children's own experience and will be matched to the stages of their development. Recording will be an integral part of the work performed at all stages.

Advantage will be taken of the strong links between Science and other subjects, in particular Mathematics, where ordering, grouping, pattern, symmetry and similarity have relevance to the living world and conservation of length, mass/weight, volume/capacity have relevance to materials and where mathematical work on distance, speed and time and reliance on graphical and other pictorial representations such as plans, charts, line and block graphs, histograms and tables all have an important part to play in science education.

<u>The Secondary School 11-16</u>

All pupils during their Science courses at secondary school and at levels appropriate to their age, ability and aptitude will study the following

1. The human body and its functioning. Human development. Basic requirements for health, personal and community welfare.

2. The functioning, needs and utilisation of animals and plants.

3. The material and energy cycles in nature.

4. The community of life and the importance of ecology.

5. The development of life. The significance of genetics in variation and evolution.

6. The forms in which important materials are found in nature and their utilisation by man.

7. The three basic states of matter, their properties, measurement and inter-conversion.

8. Techniques of handling, using and purifying materials, together with basic safety instructions.

9. The classification and properties of important chemical materials. Simple theories and models of their nature and properties.

10. The effect of chemical change in the production of new substances and of energy.

11. The different forms of energy and its conservation. Practical application of energy forms - mechanical, heat, light, sound, magnetism and electricity.

12. The action of various forces, their measurement and the measurement of their effects, especially a study of motion.

13. The place of the earth in the solar system and of the solar system in relation to the universe. The application of basic scientific principles to man's activities in space.

14. The basic principles of electronics and microelectronics based on practical work with simple systems. Their application to everyday life.

All pupils will be introduced to an understanding of the following words:

Absorption	Invertebrate
Acceleration	Ion
Acid	Kinetic energy
Activity	Liquid
Alkali	Mass
Animal	Metal
Atom	Molecule
Base	Momentum
Carbohydrate	Non-metal
Cell	Osmosis
Change of State	Parasite
Combustion	Photosynthesis
Conservation	Plant
Crystal	Potential energy
Decomposition	Power
Density	Pressure
Digestion	Protein
Diffusion	Reaction
Electrolyte	Reflection
Electron	Refraction
Enzyme	Reproduction
Equation	Salt
Evolution	Saprophyte
Fat	Solid
Fertilization	Sterile
Food Chain	Synthesis
Force	Temperature
Gas	Velocity
Genetics	Vertebrate
Heredity	Vitamin
Hormone	Wave
Interference	Work

The First, Second and Third Years

All pupils will follow a balanced science course including the foundation elements of physics, chemistry and biology, and will be encouraged

(a) to develop as clear an understanding as possible of the nature of these three traditional sciences and of any other science groupings open to them,

and

(b) to widen their interests towards other scientific areas such as astronomy and geology.

The Fourth and Fifth Years

All pupils will, depending on ability, follow

(a) at least one of the main Sciences, Chemistry, Physics or Biology leading to the General Certificate of Education or the Certificate of Secondary Education;

or

(b) an integrated course of Science leading to the General Certificate of Education or the Certificate of Secondary Education;

or

(c) a practically based Science course building up on the main themes of Science in the first three years emphasising the application of Science.

CRAFT DESIGN AND TECHNOLOGY

All children throughout their time at primary and secondary school will have the opportunity through practical experience to develop to the limit of their ability skills required during the process of designing and making things and a fundamental grasp of the essential concepts involved in this including the application of skills acquired from other subject studies.

Aims

    (a) The creation of an awareness of technology and its role in society.

    (b) The development of creativity, ingenuity and perseverance.

    (c) The development of practical skills for work of a personal interest.

    (d) An awareness of safety needs and the damaging effect on the environment of some forms of technology.

The Primary School 5-11

All children will be encouraged to handle as great a variety of materials as possible with a view to discovering their properties, to construct simple functional and decorative articles, and to undertake simple experiments in technological design.

The Secondary School 11-16

All secondary schools will offer their pupils the opportunity of continuing the progress made in the primary school through a syllabus structured to provide for the years between 11 and 16 a steady improvement in the following skills in craft design and technology.

Acquisition of Skills

    (i)   The initial preparation, shaping, joining and finishing of metals, woods, plastics and other appropriate materials using both hand and machine tools.

(ii)   The use of more specialised materials and tools for construction or assembly skills as in building and motor engineering.

(iii) The successful application of the aesthetic effect of shape, texture and colour in making both functional and non-functional articles.

(iv)   The ability to communicate graphically in styles related to the practical work of designing and making.

(v)   The ability to do simple research and to write down a logical series of actions leading to a design brief.

(vi)   An understanding of the basic principles of mechanics (static, dynamic, pneumodynamic and hydrodynamic).

(vii) A knowledge of energy sources, their generation and harnessing to be used for control purposes.

(viii) The designing and application of simple electric, electronic and micro-electronic circuits, including the use of computer programmes for the purpose of control.

Design

Pupils will undertake design-and-making projects of the following suggested kinds:

(i)   bridges, aeroplanes, high level cranes to give maximum strength properties using the minimum of materials;

(ii)   small working models of vehicles, fork-lifts etc. powered by a variety of energy sources and control devices;

(iii) small working models designed to apply the principle of velocity ratio using levers, pulleys and gears;

(iv)   electronically controlled light signalling devices;

(v)   household objects having a high proportion of aesthetic value.

Support Studies

These studies which will be mainly of a socio/economic nature will be undertaken to widen the horizon into the social/workaday world and will include:

(i)   the availability and extraction of fundamental world resources;

(ii)   the impact of technology on the individual, society and the environment;

(iii)   technology in food production, shelter and health;

(iv)   communication;

(v)   the efficiency of corporations;

(vi)   practical contact with the world of work (industrial links).

All schools will offer courses leading to the G.C.E. and the Certificate of Secondary Education.

HOME ECONOMICS

All pupils throughout their time at primary and secondary school will have the opportunity to study Home Economics which deals with the knowledge and skills which go into making a good home.

The Primary School 5-11

In primary school the study of Home Economics will centre on cooking and needlecraft. Both introduce boys and girls to basic skills such as weighing, measuring, timing and co-ordination and stimulate interest in making and creating.

Work with food at this stage will aim to

(a) promote sound food habits and ideas

(b) introduce basic understanding of the rules for safety and hygiene

(c) stimulate enquiry into the origin of foods and living patterns of other cultures

(d) introduce and develop creative ideas and themes

(e) encourage the development of concepts and skills related to other areas of the curriculum

(f) promote good social training

(g) lead to an appreciation of the value of an end product.

The handling of fabrics and articles, the enjoyment of toys and the practical use of garments, are daily experiences of young children. Needlecraft provides opportunities for an increase in learning experiences for both boys and girls throughout the primary age range. Work in this area will aim to

(a) foster work skills and techniques which can be used throughout life

(b) foster enjoyment in the experience of colour and texture

(c) help children to appreciate the quality and beauty of well made and well designed objects and the artistry and craftsmanship of others

(d) ensure success of some kind for each ability through producing an end product.

Donald Naismith

The Secondary School 11-16

All pupils during their time at secondary school will follow courses covering the following areas

(a) the home and the family

(b) food and nutrition

(c) textile studies

(d) health and safety

(e) consumer education

(f) child and human development

(g) resource management.

All pupils at the end of their time at secondary school should, through their study of Home Economics and within the context of the home and the family, be able to

(a) discuss the effect of environmental and social changes on the home, family and the community

(b) show that they can organise their energy, time and resources effectively in a variety of situations

(c) show knowledge of the physical and emotional requirements for the development of the healthy individual

(d) form opinions about the responsibilities of family life, the relationship between parents and children and other members of the family and between the family and the community

(e) understand the factors involved in human reproduction and the development of the young child

(f) understand the needs of young children and the problems of stress, deprivation and child abuse

(g) carry out and organise the basic cleaning of home and clothes and establish good kitchen, household and personal hygiene

(h) use domestic equipment correctly and safely, follow instructions which are presented in technical language and locate and identify reliable sources of information and help

(i) know the needs of safety in the home, the importance of the prevention of accidents and the principles of first aid

(j) undertake elementary household repairs

(k) prepare meals, have an understanding of the foods most in use and of the need to eat sensibly

(l) undertake household budgeting, shopping and the storage of food and materials

(m) identify specific manmade and natural fibres and show an understanding of the construction and properties of selected fabrics

(n) select designs and fabrics suitable for specific requirements and have a sense of style

(o) demonstrate competence in the manipulative skills required to make up chosen fabrics

(p) plan and carry out some original work in the field of fashion, creative design or furnishings.

All schools prepare pupils for examination in the General Certificate of Education and the Certificate of secondary Education in Home Economics, Fabrics and Fashion, and Child Development.

BUSINESS STUDIES

All pupils in secondary schools need to gain an understanding of the economic base of our society and the importance to Britain of the wealth creating process. For many pupils this understanding will be gained from the school's Preparation for Adult Life programme and from work in Social Studies. For other pupils it will be appropriate to follow a Business Studies course in the fourth and fifth years leading to an external qualification. All secondary schools provide such a course, where the emphasis is placed on learning about the running of a business rather than the acquisition of clerical skills.

Schools may prepare pupils for typewriting and office practice examinations, athough most of this work is undertaken in sixth forms and the colleges which are able to provide the range of modern equipment necessary to train students to work in up-to-date conditions.

Closely related to Business Studies is the growing importance of Information Technology.

INFORMATION TECHNOLOGY

(INCLUDING COMPUTER STUDIES: COMPUTER APPRECIATION: LIBRARY STUDIES: COMMUNICATION STUDIES)

The micro-electronic revolution has already had a great effect on the working and leisure activities of many people, but this is insignificant compared to the impact which will be felt when business machines, computers, telecommunication devices and domestic equipment become more compatible and interconnected.

The Education Committee accept that in the face of these developments all children must be taught to understand the causes and effects of these changes so that they can make informed choices relating to their further study, retraining, employment or enjoyment, and in particular so that they should be able to take advantage of new styles of distance learning, made possible by the micro-electronic revolution, such as the Open University and the Open Tech.

To this end Information Technology will be included in the curriculum of all pupils either by incorporating it in other subject areas, which will be the method most usually found in primary school, or by setting aside specific lessons.

It is the Education Committee's policy that all children leaving school at 16 should

(a) have a practical awareness of what characterises information processing - including control technology - and the use of computer-based information systems;

(b) be aware of major developments in technology affecting communication of information;

(c) have experienced the use of modern communication devices and systems in some worthwhile way;

(d) have used computers to perform useful activities which would have been unduly tedious otherwise and hence developed a practical understanding of problem solving using computers;

(e) have sufficient familiarity with common electronic communication systems to have no irrational fear of them;

(f) have developed the understanding and confidence to use Information Technology to enrich their everyday lives;

(g) have developed a basic understanding of the principles underlying information technology so that they can cope with changes in technology.

Primary School 5-11

All pupils will be introduced to Information Technology during their time at primary school with the intention that by the age of 11 most pupils should be able to

(a) use four function electronic calculators with confidence;

(b) operate a microcomputer confidently to load and run programs;

(c) understand simple ideas about the sensible and safe use of domestic appliances;

(d) describe the basic principles of the telephone system so that they could use it if necessary;

(e) use confidently any other items of educational technology which may help them in their future studies.

Secondary Schools 11-16

Education in Information Technology will be continued in all secondary schools with the aim that by the age of 16 most pupils should

(a) be able to operate a micro-computer with confidence to perform a variety of useful tasks;

(b) be aware of the variety of methods currently used to store, retrieve and manipulate information;

(c) be aware of the implications of the convergence of the methods in (b) for work, leisure and social organisation;

(d) be able to use the full facilities of the school and public lending and reference libraries;

(e) know how and when to retrieve information from electronic information retrieval systems such as viewdata, videotext and videotex systems;

(f) understand descriptions of domestic information devices so that they can make sensible decisions about the usefulness of such devices for their own purposes and operate such devices safely;

(g) have sufficient keyboard skills so that they can usefully edit their own text using word processing or text editing programs;

(h) be able to use the telephone system, including directories and directory enquiries, for work or leisure;

(i) know enough about methods of reproducing printed materials to be able to decide on the appropriate methods to use for work and social activities;

(j) use a computer system to solve relevant problems by using existing software, or be able to see that available packages are not adequate.

All pupils in secondary school will have the opportunity, where their abilities allow, of following courses leading to the General Certificate of Education or the Certificate of Secondary Education.

All pupils, including those for whom these examinations are not appropriate, will be able to follow a course leading to the Croydon Certificate of Computer Competence.

ASPECTS OF SECONDARY SCHOOL ORGANISATION

How the curricular aims outlined in this paper are carried out in practice is a matter for the individual schools themselves, in terms of curricular design and school organisation and management. All schools however, recognise the need to ensure that the courses followed during the last two years between the ages of 14 and 16 should be ones which effectively prepare their pupils either for further education or employment when they leave. For many pupils the examination courses leading to the General Certificate of Education and the Certificate of Secondary Education will be the right routes to take. For an equal number at least, however, the more directly vocational courses which are provided will be appropriate.

The pattern of secondary schooling will, therefore, generally be along the following lines.

All pupils between the ages of 11 and 16 will, throughout their time at school, undertake work in the following subject areas: English, Mathematics, Art, Music, Drama, Physical Education, History, Geography, Social Studies, Religious Education, Science, Craft Design Technology, Home Economics and Information Technology. At least one Modern European language will be studied by all pupils during the first three years of secondary school.

Within this framework it will be usual for most pupils to follow the same broadly based curriculum during the first three years before choosing from a range of options the subjects they will specialise in for the remainder of their time at school.

All pupils will be prepared for public examinations in English and Mathematics.

All schools will offer the following as examination subjects:

English, Mathematics, Art, Music, History, Geography, Religious Education, one other Humanities subject, two modern European languages, Physics, Chemistry, Biology, Integrated Science, Computer Studies, Craft Design Technology and Home Economics.

In addition schools will, where there is sufficient demand, arrange examination courses in the following:

Economics, Commerce, Sociology, Government and Politics, Social Studies, a third modern European language, Electronics, Statistics, Fabric and Fashion, Childcare, Drama, Typewriting and Office Practice.

All schools ensure that, as a general principle, all pupils are taught in classes differentiated by ability and that opportunities exist to follow accelerated courses enabling them to take their examinations earlier, where this is beneficial and is in accordance with the parents' wishes, and in some cases to transfer early to another school or Sixth Form College.

All schools offer vocational courses preparing pupils for employment and qualifications in the following occupational groupings:

1. Administrative Clerical and Office Services

2. Agriculture, Horticulture Forestry and Fisheries

3. Craft and Design

4. Installation Maintenance and Repair

5. Technical and Scientific

6. Manufacturing and Assembly

7. Processing

8. Food Preparation and Service

9. Personal Service and Sales

10. Community and Health Services

11. Transport Services

AFTER 16

The Education Committee hope that all pupils when they reach school leaving age will continue their education either on a full-time or a part-time basis in a sixth form, or eventually one of the Sixth Form Colleges which will be introduced from 1986, or at the Croydon College. Care is taken to ensure that all work undertaken in the secondary school can be continued or retaken. Opportunities available after 16 are described in the booklet "Sixteen Plus" which is distributed to all school leavers.

PUBLICATIONS

The curriculum arrangements followed in all schools in the light of this paper are described in each school's prospectus which is available to parents. A shortened version of this document is also provided to all parents.

The Education Committee hope that these publications will help to explain the work of our schools, and in so doing, enable parents, employers and other interested people to contribute in an informed way to the education of our young people which is the responsibility of us all.

ACKNOWLEDGEMENTS

This paper relies heavily on the many recent publications there have been on the subject of the curriculum. The Education Committee wishes to acknowledge its particular indebtedness to the following:

"The School Curriculum" published by the Department of Education and Science; "Working Papers by H.M. Inspectorate on the 11-16 Curriculum: a Contribution to Current Debate"; "The Primary School Survey" (H.M. Inspectorate); "A Language for Life" (The Bullock Report); "Mathematics Counts" (The Cockcroft Report).

The paper also owes a great deal to the teachers in Croydon and the Education Committee wishes to record its appreciation to them for their invaluable contribution.

APPENDIX 1

Infant Stage 5-8

At the end of this stage of education the majority, about 75%, of children should be able to:

(a) recognise and use the names of common solids and show awareness of their characteristics;

(b) recognise and use the names of common flat shapes and understand some of their attributes;

(c) work with numbers up to 100 with an appreciation of place value;

(d) perform, and practically apply, addition, subtraction and multiplication of numbers to 20, and understand the elementary concepts of division;

(e) recognise and use the coins in regular use and make purchases, giving change of these coins;

(f) estimate and measure with arbitrary and commonly used standard units;

(g) understand conservation of continuous and discrete quantities;

(h) tell the time to the nearest five minutes and state it in common ways, and use the calendar.

APPENDIX 2

Junior Stage 8-11

At the end of this stage of education the majority, about 75% of children should be able to:

(a) describe, identify, discriminate, sort and classify objects;

(b) recognise simple numerical and spatial relationships;

(c) use number in counting, describing, estimating and approximating;

(d) appreciate place value, the number system and number notation, including whole numbers, fractions, decimals, and bases other than 10;

(e) appreciate the connections between fractions, decimal fractions, and the most common percentages;

(f) appreciate the measures in common use; sensibly estimate and measure (using scales and dials) length, weight, volume and capacity, area, time, angle and temperature, to an appropriate level of accuracy;

(g) understand enough about money to carry out simple purchases;

(h) carry out practical activities involving the ideas of addition, subtraction, multiplication and division;

(i) perform simple calculations, involving the mathematical processes indicated by the signs +, −, x, / with whole numbers (maintaining rapid recall of the sums, differences and products of pairs of numbers from 0 to 10);

(j) carry out with confidence and accuracy simple examples in the four operations of number, including two places of decimals (as for pounds and pence) and 3 places of decimals (for kilograms and grams) appropriate to the measures used;

(k) approximate and check whether the result of a calculation is reasonable;

(l) multiply and divide numbers of up to two decimal places by 10 and 100;

(m) use a four function electronic calculator sensibly, to add, subtract, multiply and divide;

(n) use fractions in the sequences

$$\frac{1}{2}, \frac{1}{4}, \frac{1}{8}, \frac{1}{16}; \frac{1}{3}, \frac{1}{6}, \frac{1}{12}; \frac{1}{5}, \frac{1}{10};$$

including the idea of equivalence;

(o) use and interpret the following: diagrams; drawings; tables; simple networks; maps; scale drawings; diagrammatic, pictorial and graphical representation, statistical charts and three dimensional representation;

(p) appreciate two and three dimensional shapes and their relationships with one another; to recognise simple properties; to handle, create, discuss and describe them with confidence and appreciate spatial relationships, symmetry and similarity;

(q) read with understanding Mathematics from books, and use appropriate reference skills;

(r) write clearly, to record Mathematics in statements, neatly and systematically.

APPENDIX 3A

<u>Mathematics 11-16</u>

    <u>A.</u> At the end of the period of compulsory education <u>EVERY</u> pupil should be able to

(a) perform with understanding the four operations of arithmetic maintaining rapid recall of the sums, differences and products of pairs of numbers from 0 to 10 and use these operations to solve correctly many real problems;

(b) perform with understanding straightforward operations on simple fractions and decimals in practical situations;

(c) understand and use simple percentages in everyday applications;

(d) estimate and approximate numbers of up to four digits;

(e) use calculators accurately and where appropriate;

(f) read and understand tabulated information as in price lists and timetables; read 12 and 24 hour clocks and other combinations of dials;

(g) know enough about diagrams, charts and graphs to be able to interpret those commonly used for communication;

(h) know enough about simple statistics to be able to interpret them correctly;

(i) perform such calculations about money as are useful in everyday life;

(j) estimate and use a variety of instruments to make measurements in mass, length, time and angle;

(k) handle, create, discuss and write about two and three dimensional objects and solve problems about them physically as well as by calculation and scale drawing; interpret diagrams, plans and maps;

(l) understand pattern and proportion in shape and number;

(m) substitute numbers in simple formulae expressed as words or symbols and obtain the correct answer;

(n) understand and use ratio in everyday applications such as mixtures and recipes.

APPENDIX 3B

B. The majority, about 60%, will also be able to:-

(a) use elementary algebra as generalised arithmetic and to manipulate symbols with an understanding of what the symbols represent;

(b) construct, interpret and use formulae including linear simultaneous equations and inequalities and anadratic equations;

(c) use elementary theorems in formal and transformation geometry;

(d) use angle properties of polygons, parallel lines and circles;

(e) construct accurately bisections of angles and limbs;

(f) apply the principles of similarity, symmetry and loci;

(g) use elementary trigonometrical relationships to solve two and three dimensional problems including use of bearings and angles of depression and elevation;

(h) use a more complex calculator with trigonometrical and statistical functions, and use the memory;

(i) represent and interpret numerical information using words, symbols and diagrams;

(j) calculate and interpret probabilities and statistical data for small samples;

(k) understand and apply the basic language of set theory;

(l) represent data by matrices and vectors and manipulate the matrices and vectors to solve problems in arithmetic, algebra and geometry;

(m) represent quantities, from everyday life as natural numbers, integers, rational and irrational numbers and in standard form;

(n) use functions of one variable and be able to represent a function as a graph or a mapping.

The more able 25% of pupils will also be able to apply differentiation of functions of a single variable to practical problems.

Diversity and Choice

Proposals for specialisation at
Ernest Bevin Chestnut Grove
and Southfields Schools

A Consultative Document

Wandsworth

FOREWORD BY THE LEADER OF THE COUNCIL

Until recently the prevailing pattern of secondary education in Wandsworth - as in most parts of the country - was based on the neighbourhood comprehensive school. The idea was that such schools would cater fully for the varying needs of all the children in their locality.

I believe that this concept is mistaken educationally, and has been convincingly proved to be so over the past 30 years. I also believe it wrong that most parents should have little else to choose from than from a virtual monopoly of one kind of school. Parents, in my view, have a right to exercise real choice from a range of genuinely different schools which reflects their wishes and needs and those of their children. The proposals in this paper have, as their main purpose, widening parental and pupil choice through providing, within the Council's schools, over and above the National Curriculum, specialised courses geared up to the needs of those pupils who can most benefit from them and for whom they would not otherwise be available. The proposals also open up the prospect of specialised schools where they meet proven parental and pupil demand.

Freedom of choice is not only a basic right. It is the means whereby the higher educational standards we all seek on behalf of our children and our country's standing in the world will be achieved.

Donald Naismith

I commend these proposals to you and very much hope that they will meet with a positive response.

Councillor Edward Lister
Leader of the Council

MESSAGE BY THE CHAIRMAN OF THE EDUCATION COMMITTEE

This document is essentially a consultative document, and the emphasis rests with the word consultative. It is, I believe, couched in terms which are highly relevant to the Council's stated ideal of offering diversity of choice, stimulation, skills and imparting knowledge in such a fashion as to engage young people of today. I am confident that the proposals put forward are a major contribution to this endeavour.

I know that we are all united on equal terms in our aim to make those years of compulsory education a worthwhile background from which pupils can go forward confidently into the larger community of adulthood.

A selection process must not be seen in a divisive way, but rather as a facility by which pupils may choose the education which bests suits them.

By having such diversity of choice the Council is saying "we have what the individual needs" rather than "this is what there is to offer, make the best of it".

Donald Naismith

I commend this document as being most worthy of your detailed consideration.

Elizabeth Howlett

Councillor Mrs Elizabeth Howlett
Chairman, Education Committee

INTRODUCTION BY THE DIRECTOR OF EDUCATION

Three schools have been invited to suggest specialised courses in addition to the National Curriculum to be made available to pupils by selection so that those pupils who can most benefit from them have the opportunity to do so. The schools are Chestnut Grove, Ernest Bevin and Southfields Schools.

This paper describes the schools' response to this invitation, the means of selection it is proposed should be used, and the contribution the new specialised schools would make to the pattern of education in the borough.

If these proposals are accepted they would constitute a significant change in the character in these schools. Such a change would require the approval of the Secretary of State for Education.

The opportunity is being taken to consult at the same time on one separate proposal affecting one school only, Ernest Bevin, namely to reduce, at the Governing Body's request, the school's standard admission number, i.e. the number of pupils it is planned should be admitted each year, from 266 to 180. This will require the approval of the Secretary of State for Education.

Before the Council decides on these issues the Council wishes to consult widely in the borough and is making this consultative paper available to interested parties and to the public generally. Meetings at the three schools concerned will be held during the autumn term to explain and discuss these proposals. Details will be announced separately.

Observations and representations should be sent to me in writing not later than Friday 30th October 1992 at the Town Hall, Wandsworth High Street, London SW18 2PU. All such observations and representations will be reported to the Education Committee meeting scheduled to take place on 2nd December 1992. The Education Committee's conclusions will be reported to the meeting of the Council to be held on 9th December 1992. If the Council decides to proceed with the proposals, statutory notices will be issued.

These will provide a period of two months for representations to be made to the Secretary of State, with whom the ultimate decisions rest.

Donald Naismith
Director of Education

BACKGROUND

It is the policy of the Government and the Council, that parents should be able to choose the kind of education best suited to their children from the widest possible variety of schools. Such an ability to choose will, the Council is convinced, contribute to higher standards in pupils' behaviour, motivation, attendance, examination results and employment prospects. But there can be real choice only if parents are able to choose between genuinely distinctive schools.

Since becoming an education authority in 1990 the Council has undertaken a number of important steps to create this range of distinctive schools.

In particular, the Council:

- has supported the establishment of a City Technology College, the ADT College in Putney;

- has supported the acquisition of grant-maintained status by Burntwood, Elliott and Graveney Schools;

- is supporting the establishment of a Church of England secondary school to join the two Roman Catholic secondary schools in the borough;

- has ensured the retention of single-sex education for boys and girls;

- is establishing the country's first selective local authority "City Technology College" at Battersea.

The Council now wishes to extend this range of choice by changing the non-selective character of the three remaining county schools it maintains, Chestnut Grove, Ernest Bevin and Southfields Schools so that they will offer, in addition to the National Curriculum, specialised courses available to pupils on a selective basis.

Specialisation

As a means of widening parental and pupil choice and raising standards, the specialised courses proposed will:

- enable bright pupils to excel significantly beyond the expectations of the National Curriculum and motivate those who might otherwise be more easily 'switched off' by traditional teaching or timetabling approaches, but who would reach higher standards through following a course which engages their interests and in which they can succeed;

- have a vocational or 'applied' theme and be closely connected to the world of work: relate to and offer prospects of further education and employment through the involvement of the Further Education sector and employers. Compact Schemes - arrangements whereby employment is guaranteed in return for a proven record of meeting pre-determined targets - will be an integral part;

- offer higher levels of resourcing in terms of tuition, accommodation and equipment than can be replicated throughout the system and 'fast - track' timetables enabling pupils to progress at their own pace.

- either run alongside the National Curriculum or interweave with it and be accessible to pupils with special needs in the same way as the whole curriculum is available to them;

- encourage innovative approaches to learning and teaching. In this way they will make a significant contribution to school-based teacher training.

It is possible for schools to offer more than one specialisation. In the case of **Chestnut Grove**, the proposal is that the school should offer art and design and modern European languages; in the case of **Ernest Bevin**, science and technology with an emphasis on engineering and business administration and a range of courses in mathematics which emphasise modern applications in engineering, business and industry. A foreign language programme including modern European and community languages and Japanese and Arabic would also be introduced. Details of the proposed courses at Chestnut Grove and Ernest Bevin Schools are given as Appendix A. Other proposals for specialisation will be considered, and people and organisations responding to this paper are invited to put forward additional or alternative suggestions if they wish.

Southfields School has indicated its wishes to remain a neighbourhood comprehensive school. Its approach to the curriculum is

"to achieve excellence throughout the broad range of the curriculum, and to provide a flexible approach that follows both the traditional routes and new vocational courses. Students are encouraged to specialise from age 16 onwards in a planned progression from their 14+ courses. In addition to the usual 6th form courses students have the opportunity to follow courses in Technology, Business and Finance, and Theatre Studies."

This falls short of the requirements of the Council's policy. Notwithstanding this approach, and the fact that the school is pursuing grant-maintained status, which is not in itself inconsistent with the Council's policies towards specialisation and selection, the Council wishes to include Southfields School in this consultative exercise so that the widest opportunity is extended to all concerned for consideration of the school's future within the local education system.

Selection

Specialisation of the kind proposed means that the admission procedures of the schools concerned will need to include an element of selection since it is obviously necessary to ensure that the pupils allocated places on these courses are those most likely to benefit from them.

The Council is, therefore, making two proposals, namely:

- that from September 1994 and each year subsequently, the Council will, in consultation with the Governors of the schools concerned, reserve a number of places, a "quota", which may in aggregate be the majority of places, for prospective pupils wishing to follow each specialised course, and

- that from September 1994, these pupils will be admitted by reference to their suitability to benefit from the course, their aptitude.

These proposals depart from the schools' present admission procedures which depend, in each case, almost exclusively on how near to the school a prospective pupil lives. Pupils are now admitted without reference to their ability or aptitude.

The Council's proposals have, in principle, been the subject of extensive consultation previously and have been discussed widely throughout the education service and further afield since the Council became an education authority. The following questions are among those most frequently asked and answers are given to them here.

Is this a return to the 11+?

No. The "11+" is a test intended to measure the general ability or intelligence of pupils at the end of their primary education, round about age 11. Broadly speaking, it was used in the post-war period to decide whether a pupil went to a grammar, technical or secondary modern school considered at the time to represent three categories of education broadly reflecting young people's general ability.

The Council's proposal, described in this paper, is quite different. It is that pupils should be admitted to specialised courses or schools on the basis of their aptitude, that is, their suitability, temperamentally as well as intellectually, for the course to be offered.

Can aptitude be tested?

Yes. A variety of means have been and are being developed to assess aptitude. These include a combination of techniques such as reference to previous work and school reports, timed tests designed to identify potential, structured interviews, demonstrable ability and commitment. Such methods to assess aptitude in technology, mathematics, language, dance, art and music are well established. Details of the proposed admission arrangements for Battersea Technology College are given as Appendix B by way of illustration as far as technology is concerned.

In a number of respects it is not helpful to draw too sharp a line between ability and aptitude. Self-evidently, what a child has done demonstrates ability, in itself often a good pointer to what he or she may go on to do - potential. But an important point to make at this stage is that aptitude is demonstrated in a particular applied context and is not the same as general ability or 'intelligence', which is tested independently of a curricular context, as in 'the 11+'.

Too much reliance also should not be placed on the idea of a single "test" in the conventional sense, applied at one point in time. Children develop at different rates and in different directions. They know without anyone 'testing' them which subjects and activities they like and are good at and in which they can succeed. One of the main purposes of the assessment procedures is to identify a pupil's interest and talent as well as potential. An important part of the selection process will be self-selection, crucial to motivation - pupils wanting to belong to a particular school because they can identify with what it has to offer.

Is age 11 too soon to choose or select?

For many children, yes. All schools, however, teach the National Curriculum. By guaranteeing to all children a good basic education whichever school they go to the National Curriculum prevents damaging premature specialisation. But a considerable number of children already know at age 11, with their parents, where their strengths lie, and the kind of school where their interests are well represented and valued. Furthermore, there is no reason why other pupils, as they grow older and come to a better understanding of their talents should not seek to transfer to another school where more appropriate opportunities may exist, a preferable course of action to "bunking off", another form of transfer which is, regrettably, all too frequent where pupils are poorly motivated.

How fair will selection be?

It is important that in the event of over-subscription a decision to admit one pupil in preference to another should be fair and is seen to be fair. Scores or values would, therefore, be attached to various elements in the assessment procedures as is shown in the procedures for Battersea Technology College.

What happens to those who don't get in?

It is unlikely that this new system would give rise to unsuccessful applications for specialist courses on any significant scale, or to other pupils being unplaced for two reasons. First, as far as the specialist courses are concerned, the "quota" can be adjusted to match prospective applications, providing the local authority with an important regulator whereby supply can be matched to demand. Second, in Wandsworth's case, there are approaching 1,000 surplus places in three of the Council's maintained schools. Eventually, if, where proven demand for a distinctive kind of education such as technology persistently outstrips the number of places available, new courses and schools offering the same kind of education can be opened in response.

It may be that if demand for places on the specialist courses at Chestnut Grove and Ernest Bevin Schools are so popular the schools become wholly selective. In this event it will be borne in mind that the three grant maintained schools, Burntwood. Elliott and Graveney were established specifically as grant-maintained neighbourhood comprehensive schools, and that with Southfields, if it retains its present character whether grant-maintained or not, they cover the greater part of the borough. Furthermore, there are some 500 vacant 11-16 places in the grant-maintained system in the borough.

The question has been raised: what happens to unsuccessful pupils rejected by schools in a totally selective system. The answer is that the proposals of this paper if accepted would not lead to a totally selective system.

Whatever new arrangements are to be announced by the government for the management of the national education system, one overriding requirement will be the continuing need to ensure that sufficient school places are available to all pupils.

It should not also, perhaps, be forgotten, that where schools admit on the grounds of geographical proximity and are over-subscribed, pupils are rejected because of where they live, hardly the most intelligent basis for managing an education system, however administratively convenient.

Do these changes mean the end of the local school?

No. Under these proposals the schools concerned would admit through the quota system pupils from wider afield who would not otherwise have access to the enhanced facilities of the specialised courses for their chosen studies. The schools would, however, continue to admit pupils from their locality to follow their non-specialist curriculum according to criteria decided by the Council in consultation with the governors.

In this latter respect the governors of the schools concerned are invited to reconsider the criteria now used to decide the admissions of these pupils in the light of their own schools' circumstances, in particular, developments taking place in neighbouring schools.

Again, it should be remembered that four large schools, Burntwood, Elliott, Graveney and Southfields, with a total of almost 5,000 11-16 places offer a local non-selective education.

These proposals, do not mean that there is no place in the local system in the future for wholly specialist schools admitting on the sole basis of the suitability of pupils to benefit from the education to be offered, regardless of wherever they live. Nor does it mean that there is no future role for schools in the borough selecting on the sole basis of general ability or intelligence. The Council believes that there is a part to be played by both kinds of school if they reflect the needs and wishes of parents and pupils, and contribute to a varied, balanced comprehensive system of education. But such schools do not form part of the present proposals which are the subject of this paper.

Can the specialised subjects be offered in addition to the National Curriculum?

The National Curriculum is specifically designed to enable specialisation to take place from age 14. However, specialised courses of the kind which are the subject of this paper, which begin at age 11, would need additional hours of tuition and enhanced facilities in terms of accommodation and equipment.

The Council is able and willing to provide the extra revenue costs for the additional hours, using the powers it has under its Local Management of Schools Scheme for local authority curricular initiatives which the specialised courses would represent. The Council also has the capital resources to provide improved accommodation and equipment and is prepared to make these available.

The proposed reduction in the standard number of Ernest Bevin School

The Governors of Ernest Bevin School have requested a reduction in the school's standard number, that is the number of children to be admitted each year, from 266 to 180. This would have the effect of reducing the capacity of the school as measured by the Department For Education's Workplace Method from 1658 to 1050 and the number of places in local authority maintained, grant-maintained and the City Technology College in Wandsworth from 10440 to 9732. This provision of places should be seen against the most recent projections of demand between years 1992 and 1999 which are within the ranges of 8725 and 10366 places.

It is recommended that the Governors' request be supported on the following grounds:

- a 1050-place school accords more closely to the Council's preferred size for schools than the school's existing capacity of 1658 places;

- the existing premises are in poor physical condition and the school's large site and scattered buildings present substantial difficulties of management and supervision;

- the standard number of 180 accords more closely to the historic demand for all-boys' places for the borough.

CONCLUSION

The strategy outlined in this paper aims to:

- introduce specialisation and selection into the local comprehensive system of education as a means of raising standards. It seeks to do so through offering learning programmes more closely geared to the individual needs of pupils by widening parental and pupil choice while, at the same time, preserving the principle of equal opportunity for all;

- reconcile the need to provide communities with a good local school with the need to provide the centres of excellence required by a wider population and which would not otherwise be available. It seeks to do so by taking full advantage of the opportunities to diversify provided by the National Curriculum which guarantees a good basic education to everyone;

- avoid dependence on the principle of selection by reference to general ability or intelligence. It seeks to do so by preferring selection on grounds of aptitude, thereby allowing pupils of all levels of ability to benefit from the education most suitable to their natural interests and talents.

Invitation

Accordingly, your views, which will be most carefully taken into account before decisions are made by the Council are invited on:

- the nature of the specialist courses it is proposed should be offered by Chestnut Grove, Ernest Bevin and Southfields Schools;

- the principle that certain numbers of children are admitted to Chestnut Grove, Ernest Bevin and Southfields Schools from September 1994 by reference to their aptitude to benefit from the specialised courses offered along the lines described in this paper;

- the criteria which should be considered to govern the admission of other children from September 1994; and

- the proposal that the standard number of Ernest Bevin School i.e. the number of pupils to be admitted each year, be reduced from 266 to 180 from September 1994.

The Director of Education, who can be reached at the Town Hall, Wandsworth High Street, London SW18 2PU, (telephone 081 871 7890) will be pleased to answer any enquiries or provide any further information you may wish.

APPENDIX A: SPECIALIST COURSES AT CHESTNUT GROVE, ERNEST BEVIN AND SOUTHFIELD SCHOOLS

General

On entry to these schools all pupils will have access to tuition and facilities additional to and more specialised than the National Curriculum. All pupils demonstrating interest and ability in the schools' areas of specialisation will be encouraged and enabled to progress in accordance with their attainments and at an advanced pace wherever this is appropriate.

Chestnut Grove School

The school will specialise in art and design and modern European languages.

Pupils will have increased access to tuition and facilities in painting and drawing, sculpture, ceramics and 3-dimensional construction, fine art and print making, graphic design for commercial purposes, the history of art, photography and computer-assisted design. Pupils will be entered for the General Certificate of Secondary Education, General Certificate of Education 'A' level qualifications and the Diploma in Vocational Education.

French and German will be available to all pupils on entry. The expectation is that the school will become a centre of excellence in the teaching of modern European languages in the National Curriculum and will develop, for example, Spanish and Russian, as part of its language programme.

Pupils will be helped to develop a deeper understanding of how language works and transferable linguistic skills as a foundation for learning other European languages. An opportunity to learn Latin and its key role in the development of European languages will assist in strengthening a grasp of the structure, grammar and vocabulary of English and in sharpening the precision and logical use of language.

Ernest Bevin School

The school will specialise in science and technology within which the areas of engineering and business administration will be given a high priority. This specialist curriculum will be supported by the teaching of a range of courses in mathematics which emphasise modern applications in engineering, business and industry.

The school will offer, in addition to modern European languages such as Spanish and French, community languages including Urdu and Gujerati within its foundation programme. It will also introduce courses in other languages, notably Japanese and Arabic.

The school will continue to develop its policy for entering pupils for GCSE and other examinations when they are ready. Courses leading to a range of qualifications will be provided. These will include GCSE 'A' level, Business and Technicians Council Diplomas and the City and Guilds Diploma in Vocational Education.

The school's specialist curriculum will open pathways into medicine, engineering and the technical trades, architecture, economics, business, legal and industrial studies, public administration, business management, statistics and design.

APPENDIX B: PROPOSED ADMISSIONS PROCEDURES FOR BATTERSEA TECHNOLOGY COLLEGE SEPTEMBER 1993

Introduction

Admission to any school offering a distinctive education such as Battersea Technology College should be such as to ensure that, as far as possible, those admitted will benefit from the particular kind of education offered, and that the character of the school is preserved. The overriding purpose must be to ensure that the talents and enthusiasm of the pupils match the educational opportunities of the school.

The responsibility for deciding which applicants would best benefit from attending Battersea Technology College rests with the school authorities. Such decisions will be consistent with the Council's admission policies.

Battersea Technology College will deliver a distinctive education with a pronounced emphasis on technology. All applicants will therefore be required to take a test of technological aptitude as described below.

The Test's Criteria

The test of technological aptitude will reflect the following criteria:

- the test will enable pupils to demonstrate their aptitude for design and technology;

- the test will be objective and defensible;

- the test will be distinct from tests of general ability, and will select pupils across the full range of general ability;

- as far as possible the test will not disadvantage pupils who have received a restricted technology curriculum in the primary school;

- the test will be user-friendly and should be a positive experience enjoyed by pupils.

The Administration of the Test

A day will be set aside in the spring term 1993 outside normal hours, on which all applicants have the opportunity to be introduced to the College, will take part in interviews, complete standardised tests, and present portfolios and previous school records, which in time, will include the results of National Curriculum assessments.

Pupils will arrive in groups from each primary school. The test will start with a brief settling period during which pupils discuss a technological artefact. Next, pupils have a short teaching session, view a video and visit an exhibition, all of which are related to an aspect of design and technology in a particular context. This is followed by a 20 minute interview for each pupil with a senior member of staff at the school. Pupils are asked five questions related to the teaching session, the video and the exhibition to elicit their understanding of design and technology. These questions are closely scripted to ensure all applicants receive equal treatment. Pupils can be prompted, but all prompts are given at the same level, recorded and taken into account in the scoring procedure. All these procedures will be conducted by trained staff. Scores on the test will be statistically analysed and moderated to ensure consistency.

All applicants will also complete the National Foundation for Educational Research (NFER) Abstract Reasoning Test 1A. The aim of this test is to assess a pupil's general ability. Applicants from Wandsworth's primary schools will already have completed the test in their primary school as part of the Council's assessment programme. Applicants from out-borough primary schools will be required to complete the test during the selection day.

This measurement of ability will serve as an indicator of the make-up of the College's intake. It will not form part of the selection criteria which will be based on the test of technological aptitude.

The Selection Criteria

All applicants will complete the test of technological aptitude. The test is independent of ability measured by any other standard, and will thus ensure the admission of pupils across the range of general ability. Scores on the test can range from 0 to 140 points.

A fixed number of points will be added to a pupil's score if the applicant either (i), has a sibling attending the school in September 1993, or (ii), resides in the Battersea electoral ward. The number of points will be determined by a weighting applied to the mean test score. The weighting for the sibling criteria will be set at 50% of the mean test score. The weighting for the Battersea area criteria will be set at 25% of the mean test score. If an applicant fulfils both criteria a 75% weighting would apply.

For example, let us assume the mean score on the technology test is 50. In this case pupils with siblings attending the school would have 25 points added to their score. Pupils residing in the Battersea electoral ward would have 12.5 points added to their score.

Following the steps outlined above each child will have a total score. Places will be offered to those pupils who, in the light of the evidence produced by the assessment procedures, demonstrate that they can benefit from the education to be offered. Where the number of qualifying applications exceed the admissions limit of 150, the College will select the 150 applicants with the highest total score.

Parents' Involvement

Parents will be invited for interview. Importance will be attached to the parents and prospective pupils' enthusiasm, willingness to take advantage of the education offered and to continue full-time education or training up to age 18; in other words, commitment. Such an interview will not form part of the selection criteria.

Equal Opportunities

Suitable arrangements for applicants with special needs will be made with prior notification.

The Council will monitor the ability, ethnic group and gender of all applicants to the College to ensure that candidates are selected in line with the Council's equal opportunities policies.

Review of Procedures

The selection procedure will be reviewed annually, and may be revised in the light of review.

ACKNOWLEDGEMENTS

This book would not have been possible without the invaluable help of Jenny Fieldgrass and my granddaughter, Poppy, to whom I shall always be grateful.

NOTES AND REFERENCES

I have not given the source of quoted material where this is self-evident or obviously belongs to the familiar documentation and literature of the country's recent educational history. 'As every schoolboy knows . . .' Where elsewhere the provenance is not given it is because, regrettably, over the years, although the words have stuck in my mind, where they came from has not, a failing I hope forgivable in a work of reminiscence. Wherever possible I have been anxious to indicate where words are not my own. My apologies to unacknowledged originators and to the reader.

I particularly wish to record my indebtedness to Margaret Thatcher's record of *The Downing Street Years*, and the autobiographies of John Major and Kenneth Baker; Malcolm Balen's *Kenneth Clark* and Andrew Denham and Mark Garnett's *Keith Joseph*. Nicholas Timmins' entertaining and masterful biography of the welfare state, *The Five Giants*, was an invaluable aide-memoire as was Derek Gillard's website, Education in England (www. educationengland.org.uk/history).

PREFACE

[1]   Bernard Donoughue: Senior Policy Advisor to James Callaghan, the author of his Ruskin College Speech

[2]   Words spoken by the Labour education spokesman during a motion of no confidence in Croydon's education service at the last council meeting I attended. The motion was lost by 24 votes to 36.

3   In the case of Richmond, no minutes of the education committee for this period exist. They were weeded out, I am told, by a newly appointed archivist! Papers relating to the Croydon Curriculum are nowhere to be found. Wandsworth's records, being more recent. are in better shape. Thank goodness for newspapers.

INTRODUCTION

1   James Hanson was the driving force behind Bradford's school board for most of its thirty-year existence. Dedicated to the cause of education throughout his life, he 'was anxious to make the Bradford schools models for emulation to all the country'. At the final meeting of the school board the chairman paid this tribute: 'Of the men who have taken a prominent part in the important work of changing the character of Bradford from one of dense ignorance to that of being one of the pioneer educational forces in the country, I place, first and foremost, my old friend James Hanson.'

      In describing Bradford's record I relied heavily on *Education in Bradford 1870-1970* published by the city's Educational Services Committee to commemorate the centenary of the 1870 Education Act.

      One of Bradford's Higher Grade Schools was named after James Hanson. It was with some satisfaction that I discovered that the Master of my Cambridge college, Clare, Sir Henry Thirkill, had started his career there as a student teacher. He was fond of reminiscing with those who shared the same background. One winter, he told me, when the banks of the Cam had broken, flooding his wine cellar up to his waist, he wondered how, if not rescued, the circumstances of his demise would be received in his native city. The high watermark of his career, he called it.

2   The opinion of Sir George Kekevitch, Secretary to the Board of Education established in 1900 to supervise the national system, explaining Bradford's continuing difficulties as an education authority with the government.

3   Meriel Vlaeminke's admirable *The Higher Grade Schools: A Lost Opportunity* reminds us of the heavy consequences of yet another wrong turning when taken by an over-centralised system.

4   Bernard Ingham: Margaret Thatcher's influential Chief Press Secretary.

5   Not as revolutionary as was thought at the time. The debates and literature about the nature of a national education system in the 19th century were shot through with commercial references. Sir Keith would have readily

recognized Sir Robert Lowe's proposal to challenge what he saw as 'a system of bounties and protection' with 'a little free trade.' As Vice-President of the Committee of the Council on Education, Robert Lowe was responsible for the Revised Code of 1862 which introduced the system of 'payment by results': yet another Wykehamist!

[6] Oliver Letwin: prominent Conservative theorist and politician, quoted in Nicholas Timmins' *The Five Giants*.

[7] Nicholas Timmins himself.

[8] Gimcrack building housing the department of education and science

CHAPTER ONE: THE NATIONAL BACKGROUND

[1] Quoted in Kenneth O Morgan's *Callaghan: A Life*.

[2] The claim of Edward Heath's Chancellor of the Exchequer, Anthony Barber.

[3] Sir Amherst Selby-Bigge, Secretary to the Board of Education.

CHAPTER TWO: RICHMOND UPON THAMES 1974-1980

[1] The view of the Board of Education reporting in 1908.

[2] In tripartite terminology 'applied science' and courses geared up to those 'who dealt more readily with concrete things than ideas'.

[3] Sir Robert Morant: first Permanent Secretary of the Board of Education, whose Regulations issued in 1904 provided the framework for the national system until the 1944 Act and whose influence extended long after that; widely regarded as being responsible for the system's failure to recognize the importance of vocational studies.

[4] A characteristic view of the purpose of education as seen by Sir Robert Morant.

[5] As the Inner London Education Authority was usually referred to solely by its acronym, where I have referred to it as such I have omitted the definite article.

[6] To this amalgamation I planned to add the nearby Margaret Macmillan Teacher Training College to create a single Further and Higher Education College along polytechnic lines in the Great Horton district of the city

where all three colleges and the university were located, a move scuppered by Margaret Thatcher as education secretary.

CHAPTER THREE: CROYDON 1980-1988

1 A shorthand way to describe the size of a school, found by multiplying the number of 'forms of entry', each consisting of 30 pupils, by the number of years a school covers.

2 *Secretary of State for Education and Science v Tameside Metropolitan Borough Council* (1976).

3 Taken from Kenneth Baker's *The Turbulent Years*.

4 Cyril Taylor: knighted 1989; appointed GBE 2003.

5 Kenneth Baker, *The Turbulent Years*.

6 *Sim v Rotherham Metropolitan Borough Council and Other Actions* (1986).

7 *Regina v Croydon London Borough Council (1986)*.

8 A stirring and readable government publication describing educational problems in the United States, similar to our own, and of possible solutions, issued by Bill Bennett, the United States' education secretary between 1985 and 1988. His right-wing prescriptions for improvement closely followed much of the marketeers' agenda here. He did not know, I think, what to make of the idea of a national curriculum. He was clearly attracted by its potential to reinforce Anglo-Saxon culture, but was aware how it cut across the independence of the 'charter schools' he advocated. At a meeting he was asked which English language classics he would include in required reading. His answer: 'The Holy Bible, yuurr William Shakespeare and-with a note of triumph-our Huckleberry Finn!'.

9 Bernard Donoughue.

10 The complaint of Bob Dunn, junior education minister, mentioned in Kenneth Baker's autobiography.

11 Principally quoted here, HM Inspectorate's *A View of the Curriculum* (1980) and the DES's riposte *The School Curriculum* (1981).

12 The despairing verdict of the House of Commons' Committee on Education, Science and the Arts.

13 Infuriating example of an exercise in historical empathy taken from RF MacKenzie's inspirational but maddening book *Escape from the Classroom*.

14 Description of a proper history lesson taken from the screenplay of Lindsay Anderson's joyously subversive film *If*, filmed at Cheltenham College.

15 Jean Piaget, whose influential theories about child development fuelled much of the English 'progressive' educational revolution, studied molluscs in his early career.

16 Sentimental cinematic portrayals: Robert Donat as Mr Chips; Miss Brodie in her prime.

17 Department of Education and Science Circular 6/81

18 Ted Wragg: well-known educationalist; popular and prolific writer and broadcaster; fierce opponent of any 'outside' interference in educational matters; strong supporter of the better aspects of 'progressive' education.

19 Emily Blatch: one of John Patten's junior ministers; she fielded much of the unions' opposition to the government's policies towards the curriculum and assessment.

20 Lord Beloff: Conservative activist and writer on educational and constitutional matters, who should not be expected to be making revolutionary interventions

21 'Sir,

You are right in thinking that the idea of 'crown schools', along with many other kites being flown, will not tackle the underlying problems facing the education system in this country (leader, April2.)

You are also right in identifying three of these difficulties: a curriculum out of touch with the needs of society which increasingly needs to live by its wits to make a living; a curriculum which fails to offer the prospect of worthwhile achievement to the great majority of youngsters; and a system of management which continues to spend ever increasing sums of money without being able to guarantee to everyone basic decent conditions for learning in terms of buildings, equipment, materials and salaries.

The answers, in my view, lie in the following measures. First, the Government, representing the widest interests of society, should accept a more open and direct responsibility for what is taught in schools and for its cost, and unite the service behind a national curriculum in tune with the needs of the community as a whole. Only Government can do this.

Second, a more determined effort should be made to identify the levels of attainment most children should reach in key subjects at certain stages of their development and a duty placed on the education service to achieve them. Everyone talks about standards, but few have any idea what these are.

Third, the system of administering the education service at local and national level should be reformed to establish a direct managerial link between the money spent on the education service and the results which are expected of it. As things are, educational expenditure bears no relation to any educational programme.

Unfortunately, the measures outlined in the recently published Education Bill are designed to make each of these aims, which form elementary provisions in the educational systems of all our main industrial and commercial competitors virtually impossible to achieve.

I am, Sir,

Your obedient servant,

Donald Naismith'

22 Lord Stewart of Fulham: briefly, secretary of state for education and science in Harold Wilson's government, 1964-5, who should have been making revolutionary interventions. But such were the times.

23 The Education (No. 2 Act) 1986

24 Now Lord Patten, then briefly a junior education minister in 1985.

25 Peter Wilby: prominent educational journalist and commentator.

26 Highbury Grove: comprehensive school run on 'traditional' lines by its headmaster, Rhodes Boyson, later junior education minister and leading marketeer; St Joseph's College, well-regarded Roman Catholic school in Croydon, frequently held up by Stuart Sexton as a model institution.

27 Section 28 of the Local Government Act of 1988 controversially forbade local authorities from 'promoting teaching in any maintained school of the acceptability of homosexuality as a pretended family relationship'.

28 County Hall: the headquarters of the LCC and ILEA, referred to here to indicate the continuity of Labour policy. I was employed as a teacher by both. There was no change in policy or outlook when the

LCC metamorphosed into ILEA in 1965. With the sole exception of a brief Conservative administration between 1967 and 1970-during which Inverliever got a grant-the LCC and ILEA were Labour-controlled throughout the years of their combined existence between 1934 and 1990.

29 Opinions taken from Derek Gillard's website.

30 Taken from Stuart Maclure's magisterial *A History of Education in London 1870-1990*.

31 Paul Beresford: Leader of Wandsworth Council 1983-1992; knighted 1990; elected to Parliament in 1992 to represent Croydon Central; since 1992 MP for Mole Valley, Kenneth Baker's old constituency.

CHAPTER FOUR: WANDSWORTH 1988-1994

1 Edward Lister: Leader of Wandsworth Council 1992-2011; knighted 2011; now the Mayor of London's Chief of Staff (2012).

2 *Milne v Wandsworth London Borough Council* (1992).

3 An illuminating opinion, symptomatic of much of the teaching profession at the time, held by Mr Terry Ellis, head of one of ILEA's primary schools, William Tyndale Junior School, which was the subject of a public enquiry into its heavily criticised performance and conduct, carried out by Robin Auld QC in 1976. The affair became a flashpoint in the national debate about the state of education in the country. Three months after the publication of Auld's report, James Callaghan delivered his Ruskin College Speech.

4 In one of my annual reports to Croydon's education committee I referred, entirely factually, to the time lost through teachers' industrial action. For this reason the Labour Group moved that the report be not accepted; a classic example of the intellectual climate of the times.

5 The conclusion of HM Inspectorate's Chief Inspector of Schools on the performance of the country's largest and most important education authority, ILEA. Extraordinary even for the all too frequent vagueness of such judgments, it was of the sort that gave powerful ammunition to those who called for more objective data, and indeed for the abolition of ILEA itself.

6 *David Hockney by David Hockney*.

7 Again, nothing particularly revolutionary here. The difficulty of accommodating the different levels of attainment reached by pupils of the same age had

been recognised from the very beginning of the national system. My Junior School (ages seven to eleven) was organised into four classes each referred to as a Standard, a ghostly reminder of the original but abandoned intention to group pupils according to expected levels of achievement.

8   Kenneth Baker's admission in *The Turbulent Years*.

9   Margaret Thatcher's characteristically straightforward apportionment of blame.

10   Margaret Thatcher's equally characteristically straightforward view of the curriculum from *The Downing Street Years*.

11   The Constable of France's wry assessment of his messengers' report that 'the English lie within fifteen hundred paces of his tents' (Shakespeare's Henry V), a popular reference which passed for a witticism among school inspectors.

12   Not for the first time. Over a century before, Sir Robert Lowe had come to the conclusion that 'inspection as opposed to examination is not, and never can be, a test of the efficiency of a system of national education'.

13   The Newcastle Commission's idea of a national curriculum given in its Report on 'the state of popular education in England' in 1861; admittedly they had different ideas about what these elements were.

14   Another of Margaret Thatcher's characteristically straightforward views, this time on testing, given in *The Downing Street Years*.

15   London *Borough of Wandsworth v National Association of Schoolmasters/ Union of Women Teachers* (1993).

16   Now Lord Ashcroft, multi-millionnaire businessman and prominent supporter and donor to the Conservative Party.

17   The 1993 Education Act.

18   *Regina v Secretary of State for Education and Science ex parte Malik* (1991).

19   Rolland d'Erceville's apercu chosen-by whom I would dearly like to know-to adorn the cover of the Spens Report(1938), one of the milestone reports preparing the way for the post-war system.

20   Now Lord True, Leader of Richmond Council.

21   Quoted by Derek Gillard.

22   Sub-heading from the White Paper *Choice and Diversity*; at last a touch of transatlantic urgency.

POST SCRIPT: UNFINISHED BUSINESS

1   The dismissal by Alan Johnson, education secretary in the Blair government, of unions' lobbying to abandon assessment.

2   See Christopher Hill's *The Intellectual Origins of the English Revolution,* one of the best studies of England's unofficial, but in some surprising respects, highly effective education system in the seventeenth century.

3   Suzanne Mettler's *Soldiers to Citizens. The G.I. Bill and the Making of the Greatest Generation* testifies to the practicality of vouchers and the beneficial contribution, not only in financial terms, they can make to an education system, in this case that of the United States.

4   William Forster's modest description of the purpose of his momentous Act, a fitting note on which to end.

Printed in the United States
By Bookmasters